문법이 저절로

3STEP

Writing

3

Iam books

Preview

1
Writing에 필요한 문법

해당 Unit의 영작을 위해 필요한 문법사항을
학습합니다.

2
Writing에 필요한 문법 확인

문제풀이를 통해 앞에서 배운 문법사항을
확인합니다.

3
Warm Up: 표현 만들기

해당 Unit의 영작을 위해 필요한 기본
표현을 익히고 써봅니다.

4
Step 1: 문장 만들기

Warm Up에서 학습한 표현을 활용하여
기본 문장들을 영작합니다.

5

Step 2: 문장 완성하기

수식어 또는 수식어구를 활용하여 Step 1에서
만든 기본 문장들을 완성합니다.

6

Step 3: 문장 꾸미기

수식어 또는 수식어구를 활용하여 Step 2에서 완
성한 문장들을 더욱 확장된 장문으로 써봅니다.

7

More Practice

영작 문제를 통해 학습한 내용을 복습합니다.

8

Creative Thinking Activity

다양한 유형의 활동을 통해 학습한 영작 skill을
적용 및 응용합니다.

영작을 위한 학생들의 이해도를
돕기 위해 간혹 어색한
한국말 표현이 있을 수 있음을
알려드립니다.

Contents

사역동사

 Writing에 필요한 문법

1. 사역동사란?

- 문장의 주체가 다른 사람(사물)에게 어떤 행동이나 동작을 하도록 하는 동사
- 목적격보어로 동사원형을 쓴다. (주어+사역동사+목적어+동사원형)
- have, make, let

2. 사역동사가 있는 문장 맛보기

3. 사역동사의 쓰임

종류	쓰임	예문	해석
have	① 목적어가 사람이나 사물일 때 ② 목적보어로 동사원형이나 과거분사를 사용할 수 있다.	I had my sister clean the bedroom. I had my car stolen.	(사람)에게 -하도록 하다(시키다) (사물)이 -되어지게 하다
make	① 목적어가 사람일 때 ② 강제의 의미가 강함	Mom made me clean the house.	
let	① 목적어가 사람일 때 ② 허락의 의미가 강함	He let me come into his house.	(사람)에게 -하도록 하다(허락하다)

📣 Writing에 필요한 문법 확인

A. 다음 중 알맞은 것을 고르시오.

1 I had him (cut / cutting) my hair.

2 She usually lets her kids (stay up / to stay up) late.

3 He made his brother (make the bed / to make the bed).

4 I had my cell phone (fix / fixed).

5 I let my cat (jump / jumping) on the kitchen counter.

B. 다음 중 틀린 부분을 바르게 고치시오.

1 I let my dog to bark at home. _____

2 I had my friend waited for me at the station. _____

3 Mom made us to finish our homework right after dinner. _____

4 My neighbors let my play the piano at nighttime. _____

5 I had my bike steal. _____

C. 주어진 동사를 이용하여 문장을 완성하시오.

1 Gina _____ her dog _____ her hand. (let, lick)
(Gina는 강아지가 그녀의 손을 핥도록 했다.)

2 My parents _____ me _____ my toys in the toy box. (make, put)
(부모님은 내가 장난감을 장난감 박스에 넣도록 했다.)

3 I _____ my hair _____. (have, cut)
(나는 머리를 잘랐다.)

4 Mom _____ her son _____. (have, set the table)
(엄마는 아들이 식탁을 차리도록 했다.)

5 She _____ her students _____ at recess. (let, talk loudly)
(그녀는 쉬는 시간에 학생들이 시끄럽게 떠드는 것을 허락했다.)

Warm Up : 표현 만들기

English	Korean	English	Korean
airline	n. 항공사	garden	n. 정원
backyard	n. 뒷마당, 뒤뜰	holiday	n. 휴일
colored paper	색종이	journal	n. 일기
company	n. 회사	plate	n. 접시
during vacation	방학 동안	practice	n. 연습
fortunately	adv. 운좋게	regularly	adv. 정기적으로, 규칙적으로
flight	n. 항공편, 비행	soccer shoes	n. 축구화

🐚 다음의 우리말 표현을 영어로 쓰시오.

1 나는 아빠에게 고치도록 했다(make, fix)   I made my dad fix _____

2 그들은 그들의 자녀들이 보도록 허용한다(let, watch)   _____

3 그 엄마는 그녀의 아들이 놀도록 허용했다(let, play)   _____

4 Jenny는 그녀의 차를 검사받도록 한다(have, check)   _____

5 아빠는 내가 축구화를 사도록 허용했다(let, buy)   _____

6 Gina는 그녀의 학생들에게 쓰도록 한다(make, write)   _____

7 나는 나의 자녀들에게 먹도록 했다(make, eat)   _____

8 나는 나의 학생들에게 꾸미도록 했다(have, decorate)   _____

9 그 항공사는 내가 갈아타도록 허용했다(let, switch)   _____

10 나는 한 회사가 페인트칠을 하도록 했다(have, paint)   _____

🐚 **다음의 우리말 표현을 영어로 쓰시오.**

1 나는 아빠에게 나의 게임기를 고치도록 했다.

   I made my dad fix my game player.

   주어   동사   목적어   목적격보어

2 그들은   그들의 자녀들이   TV를 보도록   허용한다 .

   _____

3 그 엄마는   그녀의 아들이   그들의 개와 놀도록   허용했다 .

   _____

4 Jenny는   그녀의 오래된 차를   검사받도록   한다 .

   _____

5 아빠는   내가   새로 나온 축구화를 사도록 (brand-new)   허용했다 .

   _____

6 Gina는   그녀의 학생들에게   일기를 쓰도록   한다 .

   _____

7 나는   나의 자녀들에게   채소들을 먹도록   했다 .

   _____

8 나는   나의 학생들에게   그 교실을 꾸미도록   했다 .

   _____

9 그 항공사는   내가   비행기를 갈아타도록   허용했다 .

   _____

10 나는   한 회사가   나의 집을 페인트칠 하도록   했다 .

   _____

🐚 다음의 우리말 표현을 영어로 쓰시오.

1 나는 아빠에게 나의 새 게임기를 고치도록 했다.

   I made my dad fix my new game player.

2 그들은 보통 그들의 자녀들이 TV를 보도록 허용한다.

   _____

3 그 엄마는 그녀의 아들이 그들의 귀여운 개와 놀도록 허용했다.

   _____

4 Jenny는 항상 그녀의 오래된 차를 검사받도록 한다.

   _____

5 아빠는 내가 연습을 위해 (for the practice) 새로 나온 축구화를 사도록 허용했다.

   _____

6 Gina는 그녀의 학생들에게 매일 일기를 쓰도록 한다.

   _____

7 나는 나의 자녀들에게 모든 채소들을 (all the vegetables) 먹도록 했다.

   _____

8 나는 나의 학생들에게 색종이로 (with colored paper) 그 교실을 꾸미도록 했다.

   _____

9 그 항공사는 벌칙없이 (without a penalty) 내가 비행기를 갈아타도록 허용했다.

   _____

10 나는 한 회사가 나의 새 집을 페인트칠 하도록 했다.

   _____

🐚 **다음의 우리말 표현을 영어로 쓰시오.**

1 나는 아빠에게 나의 새 게임기를 　빨리　 고치도록 했다.

   I made my dad fix my new game player 　fast　.
   _____

2 그들은 보통 그들의 자녀들이 　숙제를 끝낸 후에　 (after finishing their homework)
   TV를 보도록 허용한다.
   _____

3 그 엄마는 　뒷마당에서　 (in the backyard) 그녀의 아들이 그들의 귀여운 개와 놀도록 허용
   했다.
   _____

4 Jenny는 항상 그녀의 오래된 차를 　정기적으로　 검사받도록 한다.
   _____

5 아빠는 　어제　 내가 연습을 위해 새로 나온 축구화를 사도록 허용했다.
   _____

6 Gina는 　방학 동안　 그녀의 학생들에게 매일 일기를 쓰도록 한다.
   _____

7 나는 나의 자녀들에게 　접시에 있는　 (on the plate) 모든 채소들을 먹도록 했다.
   _____

8 나는 　할로윈을 위해　 (for Halloween) 나의 학생들에게 색종이로 교실을 꾸미도록 했다.
   _____

9 　운좋게　, 그 항공사는 벌칙없이 내가 비행기를 갈아타도록 허용했다.
   _____

10 나는 한 회사가 　시애틀에 있는　 (in Seattle) 나의 새 집을 페인트칠 하도록 했다.
   _____

Unit 2 동명사 1 (주어)

1. 동명사란?
- 명사의 역할을 하는 동사
- 형태는 V-ing

2. 동명사가 있는 문장 맛보기

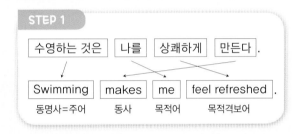

STEP 1

| 수영하는 것은 | 나를 | 상쾌하게 | 만든다 |

| Swimming | makes | me | feel refreshed |

동명사=주어　　동사　　목적어　　목적격보어

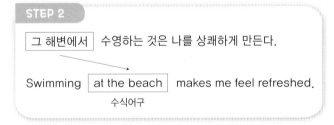

STEP 2

그 해변에서 수영하는 것은 나를 상쾌하게 만든다.

Swimming at the beach makes me feel refreshed.
　　　　　수식어구

STEP 3

그 아름다운 해변에서 수영하는 것은 나를 상쾌하게 만든다.

Swimming at the beautiful beach makes me feel refreshed.
　　　　　　형용사

3. 동명사의 쓰임

쓰임	예문	해석
주어 역할: 주어 자리에 위치하며 단수 취급한다.	Playing soccer is very fun. Learning a language is useful. Learning a language can be difficult.	-것은

A. 동명사를 이용하여 문장을 완성하시오.

1 _____ became my favorite hobby. (listen to, music)

2 _____ makes me happy. (eat, delicious food)

3 _____ helps me calm down. (draw, pictures)

4 _____ regularly is a good habit. (exercise)

5 _____ was not a smart idea. (buy, the house).

B. 주어진 동사를 이용하여 현재시제 문장을 완성하시오.

1 Playing with the cats _____ always very fun. (be)

2 Walking up the stairs every day _____ you healthy. (keep)

3 Learning English _____ very important for my future job. (be)

4 Cooking delicious food for my friends _____ me excited. (make)

5 Climbing a mountain _____ not easy. (be)

C. 주어진 동사를 이용하여 현재시제 문장을 완성하시오.

1 _____ is one of my hobbies. (sing)

2 Watching TV _____ many calories. (not, burn)

3 Driving in the dark _____ dangerous on a snowy day. (be)

4 _____ at the busy mall makes me dizzy. (shop)

5 Learning a language _____ time. (take)

English	Korean	English	Korean
abroad	adv. 해외에, 외국에	low pressure	저기압
challenging	adj. 어려운, 도전적인	quite	adj. 상당히, 꽤
childhood	n. 어린 시절	refresh	v. 기분이 상쾌하다
fridge	n. 냉장고	remind	v. 상기하다
garden	v. 정원을 가꾸다	store	v. 저장하다
healthy	adj. 건강한	travel	v. 여행하다
instead of	–대신에	useful	adj. 유용한

다음의 우리말 표현을 영어로 쓰시오.

1 수영하는 것　　　　　　swimming

2 정원을 가꾸는 것

3 영어로 말하는 것

4 해외에서 공부하는 것

5 음악을 듣는 것

6 그 빌딩의 계단들을 오르는 것(walk up the stairs)

7 채소들을 보관하는 것

8 이 영화를 보는 것

9 비행기는 타는 것

10 새로운 언어를 배우는 것(learn a language)

🐚 **다음의 우리말 표현을 영어로 쓰시오.**

1 수영하는 것은 나를 상쾌하게 만든다.

   Swimming makes me feel refreshed.
     주어   동사   목적어   목적격보어

2 정원을 가꾸는 것이 나의 취미가 (my hobby) 되었다 (become).

_____

3 영어로 말하는 것이 어려울 수 있다 .

_____

4 해외에서 공부한 것은 최고의 경험 (the best experience) 이었다 .

_____

5 클래식 음악을 듣는 것은 (classical music) 나를 도와준다 .

_____

6 그 빌딩의 계단들을 오르는 것은 너를 건강하게 해준다 (keep).

_____

7 채소들을 보관하는 것은 그것들을 신선하게 (fresh) 해준다 (keep).

_____

8 이 영화를 보는 것은 나에게 어린 시절을 (my childhood) 상기하도록 한다 .

_____

9 비행기를 타는 것은 나를 아프게 한다 (make).

_____

10 새로운 언어를 배우는 것은 유용 하다 .

_____

🐚 **다음의 우리말 표현을 영어로 쓰시오.**

1 그 해변에서 수영하는 것은 나를 상쾌하게 만든다.

   Swimming　at the beach　makes me feel refreshed.

2 정원을 가꾸는 것이 내가 가장 좋아하는 (favorite) 취미가 되었다.

   _____

3 영어로 말하는 것이 매우 어려울 수도 있다.

   _____

4 해외에서 공부한 것은 최고의 경험 중 하나 였다(one of the best experiences).

   _____

5 클래식 음악을 듣는 것은 내가 편히 쉬도록 (to stay relaxed) 도와준다.

   _____

6 그 높은 빌딩의 계단들을 오르는 것은 너를 건강하게 해준다.

   _____

7 채소들을 그 냉장고에 (in the fridge) 보관하는 것은 그것들을 신선하게 해준다.

   _____

8 이 영화를 보는 것은 나에게 그 마을에서의 (in the village) 어린 시절을 상기하도록 한다.

   _____

9 저기압 때문에 (because of the low pressure) 비행기를 타는 것은 나를 아프게 한다.

   _____

10 새로운 언어를 배우는 것은 외국을 여행하는 데에 (for traveling abroad) 유용하다.

   _____

🐚 **다음의 우리말 표현을 영어로 쓰시오.**

1　그　아름다운　해변에서 수영하는 것은 나를 상쾌하게 만든다.

　　Swimming at the　beautiful　beach makes me feel refreshed.

2　우리가 새로운 집으로 이사한 후에 (after we moved into the new house) 정원을 가꾸는 것이 내가 가장 좋아하는 취미가 되었다.

3　영어로 말하는 것이　어떤 상황에서는　(in some situations) 매우 어려울 수도 있다.

4　해외에서 공부한 것은　나의 삶에서　(of my life) 최고의 경험 중 하나였다.

5　클래식 음악을 듣는 것은 내가　매우　편히 쉬도록 도와준다.

6　엘리베이터를 타는 대신에 (instead of riding the elevator) 그 높은 빌딩의 계단들을 오르는 것은 너를 건강하게 해준다.

7　채소들을 그 냉장고에 보관하는 것은 그것들을　상당한 시간 동안 (for quite some time) 신선하게 해준다.

8　이 영화를 보는 것은 나에게 그　산골 (mountain) 마을에서의 어린 시절을 상기하도록 한다.

9　비행기의 (on the plane) 저기압 때문에 비행기를 타는 것은 나를 아프게 한다.

10　새로운 언어를 배우는 것은 외국을 여행하는 데에　꽤 (quite) 유용하다.

동명사 2 (목적어)

 Writing에 필요한 문법

1. 동명사란?

- 명사의 역할을 하는 동사
- 형태는 V-ing

2. 동명사가 있는 문장 맛보기

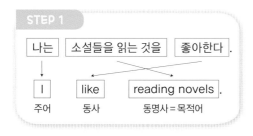

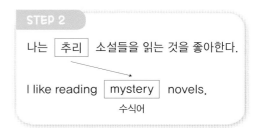

3. 동명사의 쓰임

쓰임	예문	해석
목적어 역할: 목적어 자리에 위치하며 동사 다음에 나온다.	I like listening to music.	-것을, -기를

4. 동명사만을 목적어로 취하는 동사 vs. to부정사만을 목적어로 취하는 동사

동명사를 목적어로 취하는 동사	예문
enjoy, finish, keep, mind, suggest, avoid, deny, recommend, forgive, give up, practice, postpone	I enjoy skiing in winter.
to부정사를 목적어로 취하는 동사	예문
expect, want, wish, hope, decide, promise, refuse	I want to drink water.

5. 동명사와 to부정사 모두를 목적어로 취하는 동사

동사	예문	해석
like, love, hate, begin, continue	I like going to a movie. I like to go to a movie.	나는 영화보러 가는 것을 좋아한다. * 의미의 차이가 없음
stop to V stop V-ing	He stopped to smoke. He stopped smoking.	-하기 위해 멈추다 -하던 것을 멈추다
remember to V remember V-ing	I remember to meet you tomorrow. I remember meeting you yesterday.	-할 것을 기억하다 -했던 것을 기억하다
forget to V forgot V-ing	I forgot to bring an umbrella. I forgot bringing an umbrella.	-할 것을 잊다 -했던 것을 잊다

🐺 Writing에 필요한 문법 확인

A. 다음 중 알맞은 것을 고르시오.

1 I promise (to do / doing) the dishes after dinner.

2 My sister enjoys (to jog / jogging) in the morning.

3 She kept (to ignore / ignoring) me.

4 She avoided (to talk / talking) with me.

5 I gave up (to make / making) breakfast.

B. 주어진 동사를 이용하여 문장을 완성하시오.

1 She practices _____ every day. (swim)

2 We hope _____ you again. (see)

3 Do you mind _____ the window? (close)

4 I just finished _____ the computer. (use)

5 He recommends _____ the book. (read)

C. 주어진 동사를 이용하여 문장을 완성하시오.

1 Tony remembered _____ the book. (read)
   (Tony는 그 책을 읽었던 것을 기억했다.)

2 My parents expect _____ me next week. (visit)

(부모님은 나를 다음 주에 만날 것으로 기대한다.)

3 We decided _____ the soccer club. (join)

(우리는 축구 동아리에 가입하는 것으로 결정했다.)

4 Did they forget _____ their notebooks? (bring)

(그들이 노트를 가져오는 것을 깜박했습니까?)

5 He denied _____ me last night. (call)

(그는 어제 밤에 나에게 전화했던 것을 부인했다.)

Warm Up : 표현 만들기

English	Korean	English	Korean
bark	v. 짖다	relaxing	adj. 여유로운, 편한, 느긋한
fight	n. 싸움	soft	adj. 부드러운
fresh	adj. 신선한	sunny	adj. 화창한
fur	n. 털	throw a party	파티를 열다
groom	v. 손질하다	vase	n. 꽃병
go for walks	산책하러 가다	vegetable	n. 채소
in my free time	나의 여가 시간에	wait for	-(을)를 기다리다

다음의 우리말 표현을 영어로 쓰시오.

1 소설들을 읽는 것을 좋아한다(like)   like reading novels

2 그녀의 (고양이) 털을 손질하는 것을 끝냈다(finish)

3 여유로운 산책하는 것을 즐긴다(enjoy)

4 공부하는 것을 제안한다(suggest)

5 그 큰 창문을 닫는다(mind)

6 그녀를 기다리는 것을 포기했다(give up)

7 문에 대고 짖는 것을 멈췄다(stop, at the door)

8 파티를 여는 것을 연기했다(postpone)

9 채소들을 먹는 것을 즐긴다(enjoy)

10 나와 이야기하는 것을 꺼려했다(avoid)

🐚 **다음의 우리말 표현을 영어로 쓰시오.**

1. 나는 소설들을 읽는 것을 좋아한다.

   I like reading novels.
   주어 동사 목적어

2. 나의 고양이는 그녀의 털을 손질하는 것을 끝냈다.

   _____

3. 나의 가족은 여유로운 산책하는 것을 즐긴다.

   _____

4. 나는 영어 공부하는 것을 제안한다.

   _____

5. 당신이 그 큰 창문을 닫아 주겠어요 ?

   _____

6. 그는 그녀를 기다리는 것을 포기했다.

   _____

7. 나의 개는 문에 대고 짖는 것을 멈췄다.

   _____

8. 우리는 Gina를 위한 파티를 여는 것을 연기했다.

   _____

9. 나는 채소들을 먹는 것을 즐긴다.

   _____

10. 나의 친구 Jenny는 나와 이야기하는 것을 꺼려했다.

   _____

🐚 다음의 우리말 표현을 영어로 쓰시오.

1 　나는 　추리 　소설들을 읽는 것을 좋아한다.

　　I like reading mystery novels.
　　_____

2 　나의 고양이는 그녀의 　부드러운 　털을 손질하는 것을 끝냈다.

　　_____

3 　나의 가족은 　오후에 (in the afternoon) 여유로운 산책하는 것을 즐긴다.

　　_____

4 　나는 　매일 　영어 공부하는 것을 제안한다.

　　_____

5 　당신이 　꽃병 옆에 있는 (next to the vase) 큰 창문을 닫아 주겠어요?

　　_____

6 　그는 　여러 시간 후 (after many hours) 그녀를 기다리는 것을 포기했다.

　　_____

7 　나의 개는 　현관 문에(at the front door) 대고 짖는 것을 멈췄다.

　　_____

8 　우리는 Gina를 위한 　생일 　파티를 여는 것을 연기했다.

　　_____

9 　나는 　신선한 　채소들을 먹는 것을 즐긴다.

　　_____

10 　나의 친구 Jenny는 　싸움 후에 (after the fight) 나와 이야기하는 것을 꺼려했다.

　　_____

다음의 우리말 표현을 영어로 쓰시오.

1 나는   여가 시간에   추리 소설들을 읽는 것을 좋아한다.

   I like reading mystery novels   in my free time .

2 나의 고양이는   잠자기 전에 (before going to bed) 그녀의 부드러운 털을 손질하는 것을 끝냈다.

3 나의 가족은   화창한 날 (on sunny days) 오후에 여유로운 산책하는 것을 즐긴다.

4 나는   시험 전에 (before the test) 매일 영어 공부하는 것을 제안한다.

5 당신이   하얀   꽃병 옆에 있는 큰 창문을 닫아 주겠어요?

6 그는 여러 시간 후   쇼핑몰에서 (at the mall) 그녀를 기다리는 것을 포기했다.

7 나의 개는 현관문에 대고 짖는 것을   결국에 (finally) 멈췄다.

8 우리는   어제 (yesterday) Gina를 위한 생일 파티를 여는 것을 연기했다.

9 나는   피자와 함께 (with pizza) 신선한 채소들을 먹는 것을 즐긴다.

10 나의 친구 Jenny는   큰   싸움 후에 나와 이야기하는 것을 꺼려했다.

More Practice

A. 주어진 단어를 사용하여 문장을 완성하시오.

1 my son / wash the dishes / I / after breakfast / had / .

_____

2 to release stress / action movies / helps / me / watching / .

_____

3 enjoy / on weekdays / my parents / climbing / a rocky mountain / .

_____

4 my kittens / I / play / let / on the bed / usually / .

_____

B. 다음 문장을 영작하시오.

1 나는 여가 시간에 다양한 주제의 책을 읽는 것을 좋아한다. (books on various subjects)

_____

2 개들의 사진을 찍는 것이 나의 취미다. (take photos of dogs)

_____

3 우리는 아빠가 바닥을 걸레질하고 욕실을 청소하도록 했다. (make)

_____

4 그들은 자녀들이 비 속에서 놀지 못하도록 했다. (let, play in the rain)

_____

🐚 다음 메모를 보고 Jack을 소개하는 문장을 완성하시오.

이름: Jack

취미: 자전거 타기

좋아하는 것: TV보기, 책 읽기

실어하는 것: 방 청소하기

장래 희망: 과학자

1　Jack enjoys _____ .

2　Jack likes _____ and _____ .

3　Jack hates _____ .

4　Jack wants _____ .

Unit 4 동명사 3 (보어, 전치사의 목적어)

Writing에 필요한 문법

1. 동명사란?
- 명사의 역할을 하는 동사
- 형태는 V-ing

2. 동명사가 있는 문장 맛보기

STEP 1

| 그 소녀의 꿈은 | 가수가 되는 것 | 이다 |

The girl's dream | is | becoming a singer .
주어　　　　　동사　　　동명사＝주격보어

STEP 2

그 소녀의 꿈은 | 유명한 | 가수가 되는 것이다.

The girl's dream is becoming a | famous | singer.
형용사

STEP 3

그 소녀의 꿈은 | 국제적으로 | 유명한 가수가 되는 것이다.

The girl's dream is becoming an | internationally | famous singer.
부사

3. 동명사의 쓰임

쓰임	예문	해석
주격보어 역할: be동사 뒤에 위치하며 주어를 보충 설명해 준다.	My hobby is reading novels.	-것
전치사의 목적어 역할: 문장에서 전치사 뒤에 위치한다.	Please turn off the light before leaving the room. (O) Please turn off the light before to leave the room. (X) Please turn off the light before leave the room. (X)	

4. V-ing가 꼭 필요한 표현

표현	해석
be used to V-ing	-에 익숙하다
look forward to V-ing	-을 기대하다
object to V-ing	-에 반대하다
be committed to V-ing	-에 헌신하다
be related to V-ing	-과 연관되다

🎯 Writing에 필요한 문법 확인

A. 다음 중 알맞은 것을 고르시오.

1 My job is (teach / teaching) English.

2 (Read / Reading) books isn't fun to me.

3 I gave up (wait / waiting) for her.

4 Did you lock the door before (leaving / to leave) the house?

5 We cannot go there without (buying / to buy) the tickets.

B. 주어진 동사를 이용하여 문장을 완성하시오.

1 His job is _____ cars. (fix)

2 Dad's house chore is _____ the bathroom. (clean)

3 I always take a shower after _____ in the morning. (get up)

4 My dream is _____ a writer. (become)

5 I bought a flight ticket after _____ some bonus. (receive)

C. 보기의 단어를 이용하여 문장을 완성하시오.

보기
play   travel   go   make   help

1 My best work at the company was _____ the robot.

(회사에서 내 최고의 업무는 그 로봇을 만드는 것이었다.)

2 The boy's favorite hobby is _____ with his kitten.

(소년의 가장 좋아하는 취미는 그의 아기 고양이와 노는 것이다.)

3 He always jogs before _____ to work.

(그는 출근하기 전에 항상 조깅을 한다.)

4 Our goal is _____ all over the world in 10 years.

(우리의 목표는 10년 안에 세계를 여행하는 것이다.)

5 This game's goal is _____ you to use your brain a lot.

(이 게임의 목적은 당신이 머리를 많이 사용하도록 돕는 것이다.)

Warm Up : 표현 만들기

English	Korean	English	Korean
become	v. -이 되다	internationally	adv. 국제적으로
dream	n. 꿈	leave	v. 떠나다
favorite	adj. 가장 좋아하는	lock	v. 잠그다
finish	v. 끝내다	main	adj. 주요한
fix	v. 고치다, 수리하다	make sure to V	V를 확실하게 하다
go on a picnic	소풍을 가다	motorcycle	n. 오토바이
hear	v. 듣다	without	prep. -없이는

🐚 다음의 우리말 표현을 영어로 쓰시오.

1 가수가 되는 것   becoming a singer

2 차들을 고치는 것 _____

3 게임들을 하는 것(play) _____

4 책들을 읽는 것(read) _____

5 일어난 후에(after, get up) _____

6 떠나기 전에(before, leave) _____

7 끝내지 않고서는(without, finish) _____

8 당신에게서 소식을 듣는 것(hear, from) _____

9 아침을 만드는 것(breakfast) _____

10 가난한 사람들을 돕는 것(the poor) _____

🐚 **다음의 우리말 표현을 영어로 쓰시오.**

1 그 소녀의 꿈은 가수가 되는 것 이다.

   The girl's dream is becoming a singer.
      주어   동사   주격보어

2 나의 일은 (my job) 차들을 고치는 것 이다 .

_____

3 그 소년의 취미는 게임들을 하는 것 이다 .

_____

4 내가 가장 하기 좋아하는 것은 (my favorite thing to do) 책들을 읽는 것 이다 .

_____

5 그녀는 일어난 후에 물을 마신다 .

_____

6 떠나기 전에 문을 잠그는 것을 (lock the door) 확실히 하세요 .

_____

7 그 아이들은 끝내지 않고서는 소풍을 갈 수 없다 .

_____

8 우리는 당신에게서 소식을 듣기를 기대한다 (look forward to).

_____

9 아빠는 아침을 만드는 것에 익숙하다 (be used to).

_____

10 그 간호사는 (the nurse) 가난한 사람들을 돕는 데에 (the poor) 헌신했다 (be committed to).

_____

🐚 **다음의 우리말 표현을 영어로 쓰시오.**

1 그 소녀의 꿈은 유명한 가수가 되는 것이다.

   The girl's dream is becoming a famous singer.

2 나의 일은 차들과 오토바이들을 고치는 것이다.

   _____

3 그 소년의 취미는 컴퓨터 게임들을 하는 것이다.

   _____

4 내가 오후에 (in the afternoon) 가장 하기 좋아하는 것은 책들을 읽는 것이다.

   _____

5 그녀는 일어난 후에 항상 물을 마신다.

   _____

6 떠나기 전에 현관 문을(the front door) 잠그는 것을 확실히 하세요.

   _____

7 그 아이들은 숙제를 끝내지 않고서는 소풍을 갈 수 없다.

   _____

8 우리는 아주 많이 (very much) 당신에게서 소식을 듣기를 기대한다.

   _____

9 아빠는 아침을 만드는 것과 집을 청소하는 것에 (cleaning the house) 익숙하다.

   _____

10 그 간호사는 가난한 사람들과 아픈 사람들을 (the sick) 돕는 데에 헌신했다.

   _____

🐚 **다음의 우리말 표현을 영어로 쓰시오.**

1 그 소녀의 꿈은 국제적으로 유명한 가수가 되는 것이다.

   The girl's dream is becoming an internationally famous singer.
   _____

2 나의 주요한 일은 차들과 오토바이들을 고치는 것이다.

   _____

3 그 소년의 가장 좋아하는 취미는 컴퓨터 게임들을 하는 것이다.

   _____

4 내가 오후에 가장 하기 좋아하는 것은 햇살 아래서 (in the sun) 책들을 읽는 것이다.

   _____

5 그녀는 일어난 후에 항상 차가운 물을 마신다.

   _____

6 집을 떠나기 전에 현관문을 잠그는 것을 확실히 하세요.

   _____

7 그 아이들은 숙제를 끝내지 않고서는 공원에 (at the park) 소풍을 갈 수 없다.

   _____

8 우리는 아주 많이 당신에게서 곧 (soon) 소식을 듣기를 기대한다.

   _____

9 아빠는 여름 휴가 동안 (during his summer vacation) 아침을 만드는 것과 집을 청소
   하는 것에 익숙하다.

   _____

10 그 간호사는 아프리카에 있는 (in Africa) 가난한 사람들과 아픈 사람들을 돕는 데에 헌신했다.

   _____

5 현재분사

 Writing에 필요한 문법

1. 현재분사란?
- 형용사의 역할을 하는 동사
- 형태는 V-ing

2. 현재분사가 있는 문장 맛보기

STEP 1

| 피아노를 치는 그 소녀가 | 나의 여동생 | 이다 |

The girl playing the piano | is | my sister .
주어   동사   보어
playing: 현재분사

STEP 2

피아노를 치는 그 소녀가 나의 | 쌍둥이 | 여동생이다.

The girl playing the piano is my | twin | sister.
형용사

STEP 3

| 무대에서 | 피아노를 치는 그 소녀가 나의 쌍둥이 여동생이다.

The girl playing the piano | on stage | is my twin sister.
수식어구

3. 현재분사 vs. 동명사

	쓰임	예문	해석
현재분사	① 명사를 앞, 뒤에서 꾸미는 형용사 역할 ② 명사가 스스로 진행하고 있는 일을 묘사	Look at the sleeping baby. Look at the boy sitting on the sofa. Anna is playing the guitar now.	-하고 있는
동명사	문장에서 명사 역할인 주어, 목적어, 주격보어로 쓰임	The girl's dream is becoming a singer.	-하는 것

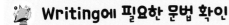 **Writing에 필요한 문법 확인**

A. 주어진 문장에서 현재분사에 동그라미를 치시오.

1 Did you see the man cleaning the windows of the tall building?

2 The boy swimming in the pool is my son.

3 I like to visit a museum showing Korean history.

4 Melting snow will make the road dirty.

5 The man relaxing on the couch is my husband.

B. 주어진 현재분사가 들어갈 자리에 체크(v)하시오.

1 The water in the kettle is making sound. (boiling)

2 The kitten is on the couch. (sleeping)

3 Look at the beautiful rainbow up in the sky. (hanging)

4 The man on stage is my brother. (singing)

5 They like to watch their dogs in the backyard. (playing)

C. 주어진 단어를 사용하여 문장을 완성하시오.

1 washing the dishes / in the kitchen / the woman / my wife / is / .

_____

2 are / lilies / floating on water / those flowers / over there / .

_____

3 that puppy / playing with the ball / only five months old / is / .

_____

4 cleaning the bathroom floor / my father / the man / is / .

_____

5 making a loud sound / the cat / scared / is / .

_____

English	Korean	English	Korean
boil	v. 끓다	on stage	무대의, 무대에서
couch	n. 소파	pond	n. 연못
dangerous	adj. 위험한	shine	v. 빛나다
duck	n. 오리	stove	n. 스토브
float	v. -에 뜨다, 띄우다	swan	n. 백조
hang	v. 매달다	toward	prep. -을/를 향해
mushroom	n. 버섯	twin sister	n. 쌍둥이 자매

다음의 우리말 표현을 영어로 쓰시오.

1 피아노를 치는 그 소녀
   the girl playing the piano

2 하늘에서 빛나는 그 별들(in the sky)

3 자고 있는 그 강아지

4 그 연못 위에 떠 있는 그 오리들

5 그 끓고 있는 물

6 그 부엌에서 요리되고 있는 그 수프

7 나를 향해 걸어오고 있는 그 남자

8 동물들 그림을 전시하는 미술관들(art galleries, show paintings of animals)

9 공원에서 노는 그들의 자녀들

10 나무에 매달려 있는 그 그네(swing, hang from the tree)

🐚 **다음의 우리말 표현을 영어로 쓰시오.**

1 피아노를 치는 그 소녀가　나의 여동생　이다.

The girl playing the piano　is　my sister.
주어　　　　　　　　　　동사　보어

2 그 아름다운 별들을　봐 (look at)!

_____

3 자고 있는 그 강아지는　귀엽다.

_____

4 연못 위에 떠 있는 그 오리들은　친구들　이다.

_____

5 그 끓고 있는 물이　집을　따뜻하게 만들 수 있다 (make the house warm).

_____

6 부엌에서 요리되고 있는 그 수프에서　맛있는　냄새가 난다.

_____

7 나를 향해 걸어오고 있는 그 남자는　나의 남동생　이다.

_____

8 나는　미술관들을 방문하는 것을　좋아한다.

_____

9 그들은　그들의 자녀들이 노는 것을 보기를　좋아한다 (love to watch).

_____

10 그 그네 위에서 노는 것이　위험해 보인다 (it looks dangerous).

_____

다음의 우리말 표현을 영어로 쓰시오.

1 피아노를 치는 그 소녀가 나의 쌍둥이 여동생이다.

   The girl playing the piano is my twin sister.

2 하늘에서 빛나는 그 아름다운 별들을 봐!

   _____

3 자고 있는 그 강아지는 매우 귀엽다.

   _____

4 연못 위에 떠 있는 그 하얀 오리들은 친구들이다.

   _____

5 스토브에서 (on the stove) 끓고 있는 물이 집을 따뜻하게 만들 수 있다.

   _____

6 부엌에서 요리되고 있는 그 버섯 수프에서 맛있는 냄새가 난다.

   _____

7 거리에서 (on the street) 나를 향해 걸어오고 있는 그 남자는 나의 남동생이다.

   _____

8 나는 동물들 그림을 전시하는 미술관들을 방문하는 것을 좋아한다.

   _____

9 그들은 그들의 자녀들이 공원에서 (in the park) 노는 것을 보기를 좋아한다.

   _____

10 그 오래된 그네에서 노는 것이 위험해 보인다.

   _____

🐚 **다음의 우리말 표현을 영어로 쓰시오.**

1 | 무대에서 | 피아노를 치는 그 소녀가 나의 쌍둥이 여동생이다.

   The girl playing the piano on stage is my twin sister.

2 | 밤 | 하늘에서 빛나는 그 아름다운 별들을 봐!

_____

3 | 소파에서 (on the couch) 자고 있는 그 강아지는 매우 귀엽다.

_____

4 | 연못 위에 떠 있는 그 하얀 오리들은 | 그 백조의 | 친구들이다.

_____

5 | 겨울에는 (in the winter) 스토브에서 끓고 있는 물이 집을 따뜻하게 만들 수 있다.

_____

6 | 부엌에서 요리되고 있는 그 버섯 수프에서 | 아주 | 맛있는 냄새가 난다.

_____

7 | 붐비는 (busy) 거리에서 나를 향해 걸어오고 있는 그 남자는 나의 남동생이다.

_____

8 | 나는 | 아프리카 (in Africa) | 동물들 그림을 전시하는 미술관들을 방문하는 것을 좋아한다.

_____

9 | 그들은 그들의 자녀들이 | 집 근처의 | (near their house) 공원에서 노는 것을 보기를 좋아한다.

_____

10 | 나무에 매달려 있는 (hanging from the tree) 그 오래된 그네에서 노는 것이 위험해 보인다.

_____

과거분사

 Writing에 필요한 문법

1. 과거분사의 형태

- 규칙 동사: 동사원형+ed
- 불규칙 동사: 형태가 일정하지 않음

2. 과거분사가 있는 문장 맛보기

3. 과거분사의 쓰임

쓰임	예문	해석
형용사 역할	I ordered a baked potato. The church built on the hill is very large. I'm really bored.	나는 구운 감자를 주문했다. 언덕 위에 지어진 교회는 매우 크다. 나는 정말 지루하다.
완료시제	They have already cleaned the classroom.	그들은 이미 교실을 청소했다.
수동태	The book is written by my father.	그 책은 나의 아버지에 의해 쓰여진다.

 참조

감정을 나타내는 분사의 경우, 명사가 어떤 감정을 느끼게 만드는 것이면 현재분사를, 감정을 느끼는 주체이면 과거분사를 쓴다.
The weather is depressing.   I'm depressed.

* 감정을 나타내는 동사: bore, disappoint, excite, surprise, interest, shock, confuse, tire, frighten, annoy 등

4. 불규칙 동사의 과거분사

동사원형	과거	과거분사	동사원형	과거	과거분사
build	built	built	send	sent	sent
find	found	found	sing	sang	sung
hide	hid	hidden	speak	spoke	spoken
lose	lost	lost	write	wrote	written

🐺 Writing에 필요한 문법 확인

A. 다음 중 알맞은 것을 고르시오.

1 English and French are (speaking / spoken) in Quebec, Canada.

2 The policeman found a (hiding / hidden) key under the vase.

3 The driver is (waiting / waited) for his passengers.

4 The package (sending / sent) from my grandmother is for my birthday.

5 Can you see the girl (painting / painted) a picture?

B. 다음 중 틀린 부분을 바르게 고치시오.

1 The math problem is very confused.

_____

2 The book *Harry Potter* is interested.

_____

3 I'm exciting about learning a new language.

_____

4 Jane was surprising at the news.

_____

5 His test result was disappointed.

_____

C. 주어진 단어를 사용하여 문장을 완성하시오.

1 Her smiling face (her face, smile) makes me happy.

2 They tried to open the _____ (lock, door).

3 We should protect _____ (endanger, animals).

4 I took a picture of the _____ (sing, girls).

5 Danny found his _____ (lose, wallet) on the street.

English	Korean	English	Korean
abandon	v. 버리다	embarrass	v. 당황스럽게 하다
break	v. 고장나다	excite	v. 신나게 하다
collect	v. 모으다	fall	v. 떨어지다
complex	adj. 복잡한	park	v. 주차하다
confuse	v. 혼란시키다	shatter	v. 산산조각 나다
dangerous	adj. 위험한	uncle	n. 삼촌
disappoint	v. 실망시키다	van	n. 밴

다음의 우리말 표현을 영어로 쓰시오.

1 무너진 빌딩들   collapsed buildings

2 버려진 개   _____

3 당황한   _____

4 그 산산조각 난 유리   _____

5 신이 난   _____

6 실망한   _____

7 그 주차된 밴   _____

8 혼란스러운   _____

9 떨어진 나뭇잎들(낙엽)   _____

10 그 고장난 문   _____

🐚 다음의 우리말 표현을 영어로 쓰시오.

1 나는 빌딩들을 보았다.

   I saw buildings.
   주어 동사 목적어

2 나는 개를 발견했다 .

   _____

3 Tina는 당황했다 .

   _____

4 그 유리는 위험하다 .

   _____

5 나는 신이 난다 .

   _____

6 그들은 실망했다 .

   _____

7 그 밴은 나의 삼촌의 것이다 .

   _____

8 그 학생들은 혼란스럽다 .

   _____

9 나의 취미는 나뭇잎들을 모으는 것이다 .

   _____

10 그는 그 문을 고쳤다 .

   _____

🐚 **다음의 우리말 표현을 영어로 쓰시오.**

1 나는 무너진 빌딩들을 보았다.

   I saw collapsed buildings.

   _____

2 나는 버려진 개를 발견했다.

   _____

3 Tina는 그 질문들로 인해 (by the questions) 당황했다.

   _____

4 그 산산조각 난 유리는 위험하다.

   _____

5 나는 새로운 사람들을 만나는 것에 (about meeting new people) 신이 난다.

   _____

6 그들은 그 선거 결과에 (by the election result) 실망했다.

   _____

7 그 주차된 밴은 나의 삼촌의 것이다.

   _____

8 그 학생들은 그 이론으로 인해 (by the theory) 혼란스럽다.

   _____

9 나의 취미는 떨어진 나뭇잎들(낙엽)을 모으는 것이다.

   _____

10 그는 그 고장난 문을 고쳤다.

   _____

다음의 우리말 표현을 영어로 쓰시오.

1 나는 꿈에서 무너진 빌딩들을 보았다.

I saw collapsed buildings in my dream .

2 나는 공원에서 (in the park) 버려진 개를 발견했다.

3 Tina는 그 질문들로 인해 정말로 (really) 당황했다.

4 그 산산조각 난 유리는 아이들에게 (to children) 위험하다.

5 나는 새로운 사람들을 만나는 것에 항상 (always) 신이 난다.

6 솔직히 (to be honest), 그들은 그 선거 결과에 실망했다.

7 그 주차장에 (in the parking lot) 주차된 밴은 나의 삼촌의 것이다.

8 그 학생들은 그 복잡한 이론으로 인해 혼란스럽다.

9 나의 취미는 가을에 (in autumn) 떨어진 나뭇잎들(낙엽)을 모으는 것이다.

10 그는 강철로 만들어진 (made of steel) 그 고장난 문을 고쳤다.

More Practice

A. 주어진 단어를 사용하여 문장을 완성하시오.

1 is used to / solving / Mom / math questions / difficult / .

_____

2 to live / their dream / by the beach / in a beautiful town / is / .

_____

3 is / my sister / the girl / chocolate ice cream / eating / .

_____

4 cannot exchange / on the Internet / I / the tickets / purchased / .

_____

B. 다음 문장을 영작하시오.

1 떠나기 전에 창문들을 닫는 것을 확인해주세요. (please make sure, before)

_____

2 그 책상에 유명한 작가에 의해 쓰여진 책이 있다. (there is, a famous writer)

_____

3 물에 떠 있는 그 백조들이 매우 아름답다. (float on the water)

_____

4 나의 업무는 그 공원에서 동물들을 보살피는 것이다. (take care of)

_____

🐚 다음 그림을 보고 [보기]와 같이 문장을 완성하시오.

[보기]
Sarah is the girl **waving at me.**

David

Lauren

Greg

James

Emma

1 David is the boy _____.

2 Lauren is the girl _____.

3 Greg is the boy _____.

4 James is the boy _____.

5 Emma is the girl _____.

Unit 7 명사절

 Writing에 필요한 문법

1. 명사절이란?

접속사 that, whether, 또는 if와 쓰이며 문장에서 명사의 역할을 함

2. 명사절이 있는 문장 맛보기

STEP 1	STEP 2	STEP 3
나는 생각한다.	Jane은 꽃들을 좋아한다.	나는 Jane이 꽃들을 좋아한다고 생각한다.
↓ ↓	↓ ✕	
I think .	Jane likes flowers .	I think that Jane likes flowers .
주어 동사	주어 동사 목적어	접속사

3. 명사절의 쓰임

쓰임	예문	해석
주어	That the Earth is round is true. Whether he is honest (or not) is important.	지구가 둥글다는 것은 사실이다. 그가 정직한지 아닌지는 중요하다.
목적어	I know (that) you are a good student. I wonder whether she will join us (or not).	나는 네가 좋은 학생이라는 것을 알고 있다. 나는 그녀가 우리에게 합류할지 아닐지 궁금하다.
보어	The important thing is that she passed the exam. The question is whether he will come (or not).	중요한 것은 그녀가 시험에 합격했다는 것이다. 문제는 그가 오느냐 안 오느냐이다.

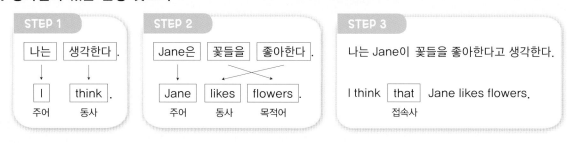 **참조**

접속사	의미	특징
that	~하는 것	주어로 쓰인 that절은 'It- that~' 구문으로 바꿀 수 있다. That the Earth is round is true. = It is true that the Earth is round.
whether, if	~인지 아닌지	I wonder whether she will join us (or not). = I wonder if she will join us (or not). * 단, if는 주어절에 나올 수 없다. Whether he is honest (or not) is important. (O) If he is honest (or not) is important. (X)

Writing에 필요한 문법 확인

A. that이 들어갈 위치에 체크(∨)하시오.

1 Do you know some large frogs even eat small snakes?

2 It's true there are many tall buildings in our city.

3 I think Cindy is the most famous actress in my country.

4 It is a fact the Earth is getting warmer.

5 It is true the novel was written by a young boy.

B. 다음 중 알맞은 것을 고르시오.

1 I don't know (that / if) it will rain tomorrow or not.

2 (Whether / If) the guest will stay in my house doesn't matter to me.

3 We believe (whether / that) it's a dinosaur fossil.

4 (It / If) is a fact that Sejong the Great created Hangeul.

5 Jane asked me (it / whether) I worked for a computer company.

C. 주어진 단어를 사용하여 같은 뜻의 문장을 쓰시오.

1 That Jon wants to be a pilot is very surprising. (it, that)

_____

2 I asked Mr. Kim whether he booked a ticket for Seattle. (if)

_____

3 I am not sure if Dad will come home late tonight. (whether)

_____

English	Korean	English	Korean
airport	n. 공항	need	v. 필요로 하다
do one's best	최선을 다하다	over	prep. -이상의
downtown	n. 시내	plan to	-할 계획이다
driver's license	n. 운전면허증	speak	v. 말하다
get married	결혼하다	surprising	adj. 놀라운
hear	v. 듣다	take	v. 데려다 주다
Japanese	n. 일본어	wonder	v. 궁금하다

다음의 우리말 표현을 영어로 쓰시오.

1 Jane이 꽃들을 좋아하는 것   that Jane likes flowers

2 Anna와 John이 결혼할 것이라는 것   _____

3 그가 우리의 도움을 필요로 하는지 아닌지(our help) _____

4 이 버스가 시내로 가는지 아닌지   _____

5 Mr. Kim이 일본어를 말할 수 없다는 것   _____

6 Tyler가 새 차를 살 계획이라는 것   _____

7 그 여자가 40살이 넘는지 아닌지   _____

8 그가 운전면허증을 땄다는 것(get)   _____

9 우리가 최선을 다했다는 것   _____

10 Tom이 그녀를 공항에 데려다줄 것인지 아닌지(take) _____

🐚 다음의 우리말 표현을 영어로 쓰시오.

1 나는 생각한다.
   ↓   ↓
   I   think.
   주어 동사

2 나는 들었다 .

_____

3 우리는 모른다 .

_____

4 나에게 말해줘 (tell).

_____

5 그것은 진실이다 (true).

_____

6 그것은 사실이니 (fact)?

_____

7 너는 알고 있니 ?

_____

8 그것은 놀랍지 않다 .

_____

9 그것은 중요하다 (important).

_____

10 Kelly는 궁금하다 .

_____

🐚 **다음의 우리말 표현을 영어로 쓰시오.**

1 Jane은 꽃들을 좋아한다.
   ↓   ✕
   Jane likes flowers.
   주어   동사   목적어

2 Anna와 John은 결혼할 것이다 .

_____

3 그는 우리의 도움을 필요로 한다 .

_____

4 이 버스는 시내로 간다 .

_____

5 Mr. Kim은 일본어를 말할 수 없다 .

_____

6 Tyler는 새 차를 살 계획이다 .

_____

7 그 여자는 40살이 넘는다 .

_____

8 그는 운전면허증을 땄다 .

_____

9 우리는 최선을 다했다 .

_____

10 Tom은 그녀를 공항에 데려다줄 것이다 .

_____

Step 3 문장 꾸미기

🐚 **다음의 우리말 표현을 영어로 쓰시오.**

1 나는 Jane이 꽃들을 좋아한다고 생각한다.

   I think that Jane likes flowers.

2 나는 Anna와 John이 결혼할 것이라고 들었다.

   _____

3 우리는 그가 우리의 도움을 필요로 하는지 아닌지 모른다.

   _____

4 이 버스가 시내로 가는지 아닌지 나에게 말해줘.

   _____

5 Mr. Kim이 일본어를 말할 수 없다는 것은 진실이다.

   _____

6 Tyler가 새 차를 살 계획이라는 것이 사실이니?

   _____

7 너는 그 여자가 40살이 넘는지 아닌지 알고 있니?

   _____

8 그가 운전면허증을 땄다는 것은 놀랍지 않다.

   _____

9 우리가 최선을 다했다는 것이 중요하다.

   _____

10 Kelly는 Tom이 그녀를 공항에 데려다줄 것인지 아닌지 궁금하다.

   _____

Unit 8 부사절

 Writing에 필요한 문법

1. 부사절이란?

시간, 이유, 목적 등을 나타내는 접속사와 함께 쓰이며 문장에서 부사의 역할을 함

2. 부사절이 있는 문장 맛보기

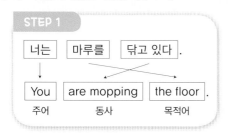

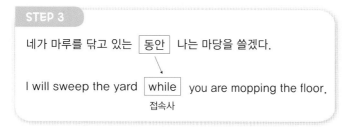

3. 부사절의 쓰임

쓰임	예문	해석
시간	When I entered the classroom, everyone looked at me. Sally was studying while you were playing outside. Kevin should finish his project before he goes on a vacation. The show will start after the audience takes their seats.	내가 교실에 들어갔을 때, 모두가 나를 쳐다보았다. 네가 밖에서 놀고 있는 동안 Sally는 공부하고 있었다. Kevin은 휴가를 떠나기 전에 그의 프로젝트를 끝내야 한다. 그 쇼는 청중들이 자리에 앉은 후에 시작할 것이다.
원인	Tyler will not arrive on time because he missed the train.	Tyler는 기차를 놓쳤기 때문에 제 시간에 도착하지 못할 것이다.
대조	The box didn't move even though I pushed it with all my strength.	그 상자는 내가 온 힘을 다해 밀었음에도 불구하고 움직이지 않았다.

접속사	의미	접속사	의미
when	~할 때	after	~후에
while	~하는 동안	because	~때문에
before	~전에	even though, although	비록 ~일지라도

* 부사절이 문장의 맨 앞에 올 경우, 부사절 뒤에 comma(,)를 붙인다.

Tyler will not arrive on time because he missed the train.
= Because he missed the train, Tyler will not arrive on time.

🐾 Writing에 필요한 문법 확인

A. comma(,)가 필요한 곳에 표시하시오. comma(,)가 필요 없다면 X표 하시오.

1 When fall comes leaves begin to change color.

2 Mom was reading a book while her baby was sleeping.

3 Even though it rained heavily the girl didn't wear her rain boots.

4 Because I didn't sleep well last night I'm very tired.

5 What do you want to do after you graduate from university?

B. 다음 중 알맞은 것을 고르시오.

1 I dress up and eat breakfast (before / while) I go to school.

2 (After / Because) I'm busy, I cannot join the party tonight.

3 Sean lost the game (even though / when) he did his best.

4 (When / After) Kate called Don, he was watering the garden.

5 Jane takes care of her little sister (after / while) her mother is washing the dishes.

C. because와 even though 중 알맞은 것을 쓰시오.

1 Penguins cannot fly _____ they are birds.

2 _____ Roy is too young, he cannot drive a car.

3 _____ the man is poor, he always looks happy.

4 The children couldn't play in the yard _____ it was dark outside.

5 Our family members gather every month _____ we live far away.

English	Korean	English	Korean
brush one's teeth	이를 닦다	go to bed	잠자리에 들다
call	v. 전화하다	grade	n. 성적
coat	n. 코트	look	v. -해 보이다
dinner	n. 저녁 식사	outside	adv. 밖에서
do one's homework	숙제하다	wash the dishes	설거지하다
exam	n. 시험	wear	v. 입다
go on a picnic	소풍가다	weather	n. 날씨

다음의 우리말 표현을 영어로 쓰시오.

1 네가 마루를 닦고 있는 동안   while you are mopping the floor

2 네가 어젯밤에 나에게 전화했을 때(last night) _____

3 네가 집을 청소하고 있는 동안 _____

4 네가 잠자리에 들기 전에 _____

5 그가 열심히 공부했기 때문에 _____

6 매우 춥기 때문에 _____

7 내가 책을 읽고 있었던 동안 _____

8 날씨가 비록 좋지 않았지만 _____

9 나의 할머니는 비록 70세이지만 _____

10 네가 숙제를 한 후에 _____

🐚 **다음의 우리말 표현을 영어로 쓰시오.**

1 너는　마루를　닦고 있다.
　→
　You　are mopping　the floor.
　주어　　동사　　목적어

2 너는　어젯밤에　나에게　전화했다 .

_____

3 너는　집을　청소하고 있다 .

_____

4 너는　이를　닦아야만 한다 .

_____

5 그는　시험에서 (on the exam)　좋은 성적을　받았다 (get a good grade).

_____

6 그녀는　코트를　입는다 .

_____

7 엄마는　저녁 식사를　만드셨다 .

_____

8 날씨가　좋지 않았다 .

_____

9 나의 할머니는　70세　이다 .

_____

10 너는　밖에서　놀 수 있다 .

_____

🐚 **다음의 우리말 표현을 영어로 쓰시오.**

1 　나는　마당을　쓸겠다.
　　↓
　　I　will sweep　the yard.
　주어　　동사　　목적어

2 　나는　음악을　듣고 있었다.

_____

3 　나는　설거지를　하겠다.

_____

4 　너는　잠자리에 든다.

_____

5 　그는　열심히　공부했다.

_____

6 　매우　춥다.

_____

7 　나는　책을　읽고 있었다.

_____

8 　우리는　소풍을　갔다.

_____

9 　그녀는　매우 젊어　보인다.

_____

10 　너는　숙제를　한다.

_____

🐚 다음의 우리말 표현을 영어로 쓰시오.

1 네가 마루를 닦고 있는 동안 나는 마당을 쓸겠다.

   I will sweep the yard while you are mopping the floor.

2 네가 어젯밤에 나에게 전화했을 때 , 나는 음악을 듣고 있었다.

   _____

3 네가 집을 청소하고 있는 동안 , 나는 설거지를 하겠다.

   _____

4 너는 잠자리에 들기 전에 이를 닦아야만 한다.

   _____

5 그는 열심히 공부했기 때문에 시험에서 좋은 성적을 얻었다.

   _____

6 매우 춥기 때문에 그녀는 코트를 입는다.

   _____

7 내가 책을 읽고 있는 동안 엄마는 저녁 식사를 만드셨다.

   _____

8 날씨가 비록 좋진 않았 지만 , 우리는 소풍을 갔다.

   _____

9 나의 할머니는 비록 70세 이 지만 , 매우 젊어 보인다.

   _____

10 너는 숙제를 한 후에 밖에서 놀 수 있다.

   _____

Unit 9 과거완료

 ## Writing에 필요한 문법

1. 과거완료 시제의 형태

주어	had + 과거분사
I	
You / We / They	had studied.
He / She / It	

2. 과거완료 시제 문장 맛보기

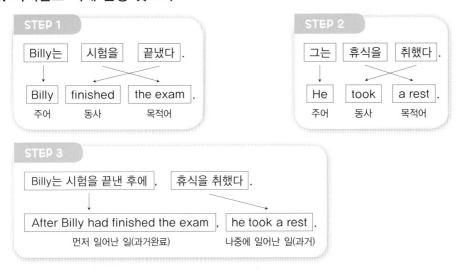

STEP 1

| Billy는 | 시험을 | 끝냈다 |

| Billy | finished | the exam |
| 주어 | 동사 | 목적어 |

STEP 2

| 그는 | 휴식을 | 취했다 |

| He | took | a rest |
| 주어 | 동사 | 목적어 |

STEP 3

| Billy는 시험을 끝낸 후에 | , | 휴식을 취했다 |

| After Billy had finished the exam | , | he took a rest |
| 먼저 일어난 일(과거완료) | | 나중에 일어난 일(과거) |

3. 과거완료 시제의 쓰임

과거 완료	예문	해석
과거보다 더 앞서 일어난 일 (대과거)을 표현할 때	After Harry had taken a break, he could start his job again.	Harry는 휴식을 취한 후에 일을 다시 시작할 수 있었다.
대과거에 시작된 일이 과거 어느 시점에서 완료되었음을 표현할 때	They had already eaten dinner when I came home.	내가 집에 갔을 때, 그들은 이미 저녁을 먹었다.

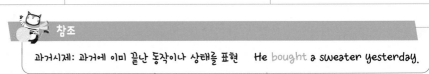

참조

과거시제: 과거에 이미 끝난 동작이나 상태를 표현   He bought a sweater yesterday.

4. 과거완료 시제의 기본 문장

종류	형태	예문
긍정문	주어+had+과거분사~.	I had seen the new student.
부정문	주어+had+not+과거분사~.	I had not seen the new student.
의문문	Had+주어+과거분사~?	Had you seen the new student?

🗣 Writing에 필요한 문법 확인

A. 다음 중 알맞은 것을 고르시오.

1 Mike (has brushed / had brushed) his teeth when I arrived home.

2 The thieves (leave / had left) the place when the police arrived there.

3 The students (have studied / had studied) for the test before they passed it.

4 Mr. Cooper (teaches / had taught) Spanish before he came to the school.

5 After David (visits / had visited) the museum, he understood the history of England well.

B. 주어진 동사를 이용하여 과거완료 시제 문장을 완성하시오.

1 The train _____ already _____ to Paris when I came to the station. (leave)

2 The couple _____ in that apartment for 10 years before we moved in. (live)

3 Justin _____ an e-mail before his boss came to the office. (send)

4 John _____ in London before he went to Paris. (be)

5 Sophia _____ the book twice before she wrote the review of it. (read)

C. 다음 문장을 과거완료 시제 문장으로 고쳐 쓰시오.

1 After Sarah stopped drinking coffee, she could sleep well.

_____

2 When I arrived in the classroom, the lecture started.

_____

3 Jason was reading the book when his mom called him.

_____

Warm Up : 표현 만들기

English	Korean	English	Korean
biology	n. 생물학	for years	수년간
box office	매표소	observe	v. 목격하다
break	v. 깨뜨리다	physics	n. 물리학
businessman	n. 사업가	spend all one's money	모든 돈을 다 써버리다
culture	n. 문화	surprising	adj. 놀라운
earn	v. (돈을) 벌다	theater	n. 극장
expensive	adj. 비싼	truth	n. 진실

🌐 다음의 우리말 표현을 <u>과거완료 시제</u>를 사용하여 영어로 쓰시오.

1 Billy는 끝냈다   Billy had finished _____

2 나는 공부했다   _____

3 Jack은 야구선수였다   _____

4 그들은 믿지 않았다   _____

5 Sarah는 구매하였다(buy)   _____

6 David는 배웠다   _____

7 Mike는 살았다(live)   _____

8 나의 개가 깨뜨렸다   _____

9 Jason은 써버렸다(spend)   _____

10 Jay는 공부를 했다   _____

💭 **다음의 우리말 표현을 영어로 쓰시오.**

1 Billy는   시험을   끝냈다.
   ↓
   Billy   finished   the exam.
   주어   동사   목적어

2 나는   그 수학 시험을   보았다 .

   _____

3 Jack은   사업가가   되었다 .

   _____

4 그들은   그것을   목격하였다 .

   _____

5 나는   그 극장에   도착했다 (arrive at).

   _____

6 David는   한국어를   배웠다 .

   _____

7 그는   돈을   많이   벌었다 .

   _____

8 나는   일어났다 (wake up).

   _____

9 그의 엄마는   그에게   전화 했다 .

   _____

10 Jay는   물리학을   공부하였다 .

   _____

🐚 **다음의 우리말 표현을 영어로 쓰시오.**

1 그는   휴식을   취했다.

He   took   a rest.
주어   동사   목적어

2   나는   수학을   매우 열심히   공부했다 .

_____

3   Jack은   유명한   야구선수였다 .

_____

4   그들은   그 놀라운 진실을   믿지 않았다 .

_____

5   Sarah는   그 매표소에서   표들을   구매하였다 .

_____

6   그는   한국 문화를   이해하기 시작했다 .

_____

7   Mike는   작은 집에   살았다 .

_____

8   나의 개가   그 비싼 꽃병을   깨뜨렸다 .

_____

9   Jason은   이미 (already)   그의 모든 돈을   다 써버렸다 .

_____

10   Jay는   생물학을   수년간   공부했다 .

🐚 다음의 우리말 표현을 먼저 일어난 일은 <u>과거완료 시제</u>, 나중에 일어난 일은 <u>과거시제</u>를 사용하여 영어로 쓰시오.

1 Billy는 시험을 끝낸 후에, 휴식을 취했다.
   After Billy had finished the exam, he took a rest.

2 나는 그 수학 시험을 보기 전에, 수학을 매우 열심히 공부했다.

3 Jack은 사업가가 되기 전에, 유명한 야구선수였다.

4 그들이 그것을 목격하기 전에, 그들은 그 놀라운 진실을 믿지 않았다.

5 내가 그 극장에 도착했을 때, Sarah는 매표소에서 표들을 구매하였다.

6 David는 한국어를 배운 후에, 한국 문화를 이해하기 시작했다.

7 Mike는 돈을 많이 벌기 전에, 작은 집에 살았다.

8 내가 일어나기 전에(wake up), 나의 개가 그 비싼 꽃병을 깨뜨렸다.

9 Jason의 엄마가 Jason에게 전화했을 때, 그는 이미 모든 돈을 다 써버렸다.

10 Jay는 물리학을 공부하기 전, 생물학을 수년간 공부했다.

More Practice

A. 주어진 단어를 사용하여 문장을 완성하시오.

1 It's / whether / a White Christmas / will have / not obvious / we / this year.

_____

2 it / a fact / James / last night / Is / had a car accident / that / ?

_____

3 Even though / is not good / will enjoy / , / the weather / swimming / I / .

_____

4 had already eaten / got home / they / , / When we / dinner / .

_____

B. 다음 문장을 영작하시오.

1 나는 Jon이 Julie를 사랑하는지 궁금하다. (wonder, whether)

_____

2 Tom은 그녀가 영국으로 떠날 것이라는 것을 들었다. (leave for England)

_____

3 Mr. Homer는 그가 이탈리아에 살았을 때 유명한 음식점을 경영했다. (run a famous restaurant)

_____

4 Sharon은 그녀가 음식점에 가방을 두고 왔다는 것을 발견했다. (find, leave her bag)

_____

🐚 다음은 Kevin의 일기이다. 괄호 안의 단어를 사용하여 문장을 다시 쓰시오.

① I came home from school. My mom was preparing dinner. (when)

② I washed my hands. I ate dinner with my family. (after)

After dinner, something happened.

③ I was doing my homework. My mom was washing the dishes. (while)

At that time, my little brother came and scribbled on my notebook in crayon.

④ He messed up my homework. I had to do my homework again. (because)

⑤ I was angry with him. But I still love my little brother. (even though)

① When I came home from school, my mom was preparing dinner.

② After _____.

After dinner, something happened.

③ I _____.

At that time, my little brother came and scribbled on my notebook in crayon.

④ I _____.

⑤ Even though _____.

Unit 10 관계대명사

 Writing에 필요한 문법

1. 관계대명사란?

- 접속사와 대명사의 역할을 함
- 관계대명사가 이끄는 절(관계대명사절)은 형용사절로써, 앞에 나오는 명사(선행사)를 수식함

2. 관계대명사가 있는 문장 맛보기

3. 관계대명사의 쓰임

대상	격	관계대명사	쓰임 및 해석
사람	주격	Who, that	Julie is the friend who gave me a doll for my birthday. = Julie is the friend that gave me a doll for my birthday. Julie는 나의 생일 선물로 인형을 주었던 친구이다.
	소유격	whose	I know a man whose job is a nurse. 나는 직업이 간호사인 한 남자를 알고 있다.
	목적격	who(m), that	The man who(m) I met on the street is my English teacher. = The man that I met on the street is my English teacher. 내가 길에서 만났던 남자는 나의 영어 선생님이다.

사물, 동물	주격	which, that	She has a huge house which has many rooms. = She has a huge house that has many rooms. 그녀는 많은 방이 있는 거대한 집을 가지고 있다.
	소유격	whose	That dog whose tail is short is so cute. 꼬리가 짧은 저 개는 매우 귀엽다.
	목적격	which, that	The flowers which my grandmother grows in her garden are beautiful. = The flowers that my grandmother grows in her garden are beautiful. 나의 할머니가 정원에 키우는 꽃들은 아름답다.

참조

* 목적격 관계대명사 (whom, which, that)는 생략할 수 있다.
  The peaches (that) I bought are very sweet. (생략 가능)
  I bought the peaches that are very sweet. (생략 불가능)
* 관계대명사 who은 주격뿐 아니라 목적격 대명사로도 사용할 수 있다.
  The man whom I met on the street is my English teacher.
  = The man who I met on the street is my English teacher.

Writing에 필요한 문법 확인

A. 다음 중 알맞은 것을 고르시오.

1 The old lady (which / whose) son is a doctor lives in my neighborhood.

2 Anyone (who / which) is interested in classical music will like the concert.

3 Tony liked the tomato pasta (whom / that) I cooked last Sunday.

4 My father caught a fish (that / who) has blue fins.

5 The children (whose / whom) I played with in the playground are my cousins.

B. 관계대명사절에 밑줄을 그으시오.

1 I like the woman who teaches me science at school.

2 Can you tell me about your new computer which you bought yesterday?

3 The movie that I saw last week was fun and touching.

4 The bus driver who took us to school is very kind.

5 The people whom I met at the mall were friendly.

English	Korean	English	Korean
delicious	adj. 맛있는	recommend	v. 추천하다
discuss	v. 토론하다	restaurant	n. 음식점
glasses	n. 안경	ripe	adj. 익은
grow	v. 재배하다	run into	우연히 만나다
interesting	adj. 흥미있는	topic	n. 주제
perfectly	adv. 완벽하게	vegetarian	n. 채식주의자
puppy	n. 강아지	win a gold medal	금메달을 따다

🐚 **다음의 우리말 표현을 영어로 쓰시오.**

1 귀여운 눈을 가진 나의 어린 여동생   my little sister who has cute eyes

2 Tom이 나에게 추천했던 그 해변   the beach _____

3 안경을 쓰고 있는 그 소년   the boy _____

4 내가 좋아하는 그 수영선수   the swimmer _____

5 우리가 토론했던 그 주제   the topic _____

6 음식이 맛있는 어떤 음식점   any restaurant _____

7 여동생이 유명한 가수인 오랜 친구   an old friend _____

8 나의 아버지가 재배했던 그 사과들   the apples _____

9 책 읽는 것을 즐기는 그 남자(enjoy reading)   the man _____

10 이름이 Happy인 강아지   a puppy _____

🐚 **다음의 우리말 표현을 영어로 쓰시오.**

1 나는   나의 어린 여동생을   사랑한다.

   I   love   my little sister.
   주어   동사   목적어

2 나는   그 해변에   갈 것이다 .

   _____

3 그 소년은   나의 남동생이다 .

   _____

4 그 수영선수는   금메달을   땄다 .

   _____

5 그 주제는   흥미로웠다 .

   _____

6 너는   어떤 음식점을   알고 있니 ?

   _____

7 나는   오랜 친구를   우연히 만났다 .

   _____

8 그 사과들은   완벽하게   익었다 .

   _____

9 그 남자는   채식주의자이다 .

   _____

10 Jane은   강아지를   가지고 있다 .

   _____

🐚 **다음의 우리말 표현을 영어로 쓰시오.**

1 그녀는   귀여운 눈을   가지고 있다.
   ↓
   She   has   cute eyes.
   주어   동사   목적어

2 Tom은   나에게   그 곳을   추천했다 .

_____

3 그는   안경을   쓰고 있다 .

_____

4 나는   그를   좋아한다 .

_____

5 우리는   어제   그것을   토론했다 .

_____

6 그 곳의 음식은   맛있다 .

_____

7 그의 여동생은   유명한   가수이다 .

_____

8 나의 아버지가   그것들을   재배했다 .

_____

9 그는   책 읽는 것을   즐긴다 .

_____

10 그녀의   이름은   Happy이다 .

_____

다음의 우리말 표현을 영어로 쓰시오.

1　나는 귀여운 눈을 가진 나의 어린 여동생을 사랑한다.

　　I love my little sister who has cute eyes.

2　나는 Tom이 나에게 추천했던 그 해변에 갈 것이다.

3　안경을 쓰고 있는 그 소년은 나의 남동생이다.

4　내가 좋아하는 그 수영선수는 금메달을 땄다.

5　우리가 어제 토론했던 그 주제는 흥미로웠다.

6　너는 음식이 맛있는 어떤 음식점을 알고 있니?

7　나는 여동생이 유명한 가수인 오랜 친구를 우연히 만났다.

8　나의 아버지가 재배했던 그 사과들은 완벽하게 익었다.

9　책 읽는 것을 즐기는 그 남자는 채식주의자이다.

10　Jane은 이름이 Happy인 강아지를 가지고 있다.

Unit 11 가정법 현재

 Writing에 필요한 문법

1. 가정법 현재의 형태

If+주어+동사의 현재형, 주어+will/can+동사원형

2. 가정법 현재가 있는 문장 맛보기

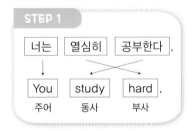

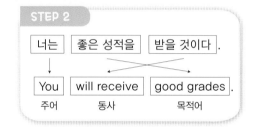

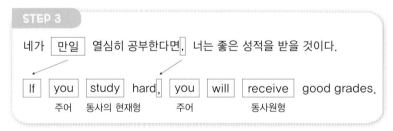

3. 가정법 현재의 쓰임

쓰임	예문	해석
현재나 미래의 일을 가정	If it is sunny this Saturday, I will go to the zoo. If Matt finishes his homework quickly, he can play baseball.	만일 ~한다면, ~할 것이다 (~할 수 있다)

참조

* Unless: 만약 ~하지 않는다면 (=If~not)

If it is not sunny this Saturday, I won't go to the zoo. = Unless it is sunny, I won't go to the zoo.

🐺 Writing에 필요한 문법 확인

A. 주어진 단어를 이용하여 문장을 완성하시오.

1 If the man _____ up, he can catch the train. (hurry)

2 If you _____ this medicine, you will get better. (take)

3 If the driver _____ carefully, he will have an accident. (not, drive)

4 If the students _____ their tests, they can't leave the classroom. (not, submit)

5 If the computer _____ too expensive, I can't buy it. (be)

B. 다음 중 틀린 부분을 바르게 고치시오.

1 Unless it doesn't rain, we will have an outdoor concert. _____

2 If Amy hear any good news, she will call me. _____

3 If you didn't know the password, you can't enter the room. _____

4 Unless we don't follow the traffic rules, we will be in danger. _____

5 If you don't exercise regularly, you didn't get in shape. _____

C. 두 문장이 같은 뜻이 되도록 빈칸에 알맞은 단어를 쓰시오.

1 If you don't miss the bus, you won't be late for school.

= Unless you _____ the bus, you won't be late for school.

2 If the swimmer doesn't practice hard, he can't win the race.

= Unless the swimmer _____ hard, he can't win the race.

3 If the children don't stand in line, they can't play the game.

= Unless the children _____ in line, they can't play the game.

4 If Margaret doesn't go to bed early, she will sleep late in the morning.

= Unless Margaret _____ to bed early, she will sleep late in the morning.

5 If you don't come to my birthday party, I will be disappointed.

= Unless you _____ to my birthday party, I will be disappointed.

English	Korean	English	Korean
cancel	v. 취소하다	office	n. 사무실
disappointed	adj. 실망한	refrigerator	n. 냉장고
enough	adj. 충분한	some	adj. 약간의
expensive	adj. 비싼	spoil	v. (음식이) 상하다
extra	adj. 여분의	stay	v. 머무르다
fix	v. 고치다	tool	n. 도구
keep	v. 보관하다	trip	n. 여행

🐚 다음의 우리말 표현을 영어로 쓰시오.

1 네가 열심히 공부한다면

   if you study hard

2 날씨가 좋다면

3 Mrs. Kim이 충분한 사과들을 가지고 있다면

4 내가 약간의 도구들을 가지고 있다면

5 Melany가 그녀의 사무실에 있다면

6 춥지 않다면

7 여분의 방이 하나 있다면(there is)

8 그 티켓이 너무 비싸면

9 내가 Sarah의 생일 파티에 가지 않는다면(unless)

10 네가 그 음식을 그 냉장고에 보관하지 않는다면(unless)

🐚 **다음의 우리말 표현을 영어로 쓰시오.**

1 너는   열심히   공부한다.
   ↓   ✕
  You   study   hard.
  주어   동사   부사

2 날씨가   좋다 .

_____

3 Mrs. Kim은   충분한 사과들을   가지고 있다 .

_____

4 나는   약간의 도구들을   가지고 있다 .

_____

5 Melany는   그녀의 사무실에   있다 .

_____

6 춥지 않다 .

_____

7 여분의 방이 하나   있다 .

_____

8 그 티켓은   너무   비싸다 .

_____

9 나는   Sarah의 생일 파티에   간다 .

_____

10 너는   그 음식을   그 냉장고에   보관한다 .

_____

🐚 **다음의 우리말 표현을 영어로 쓰시오.**

1 너는   좋은 성적을   받을 것이다.
        You   will receive   good grades.
        주어   동사   목적어

2 우리는   그 여행을   취소하지 않을 것이다 .

_____

3 그녀는   사과 잼을   만들 것이다 .

_____

4 나는   너의 자전거를   고칠 수 있다 .

_____

5 그녀는   전화를 (the phone)   받을 것이다 (answer).

_____

6 우리는   바다에서 (in the sea)   수영할 수 있다 .

_____

7 너는   거기에서   머무를 수 있다 .

_____

8 나는   그 쇼에   갈 수 없다 .

_____

9 그녀는   실망할 것이다 .

_____

10 그것은   상하게 될 것이다 .

_____

다음의 우리말 표현을 영어로 쓰시오.

1 네가 만일 열심히 공부한다면, 너는 좋은 성적을 받을 것이다.

   If you study hard, you will receive good grades.

2 날씨가 좋다면, 우리는 그 여행을 취소하지 않을 것이다.

   _____

3 Mrs. Kim이 충분한 사과들을 가지고 있다면, 그녀는 사과 잼을 만들 것이다.

   _____

4 내가 약간의 도구들을 가지고 있다면, 나는 너의 자전거를 고칠 수 있다.

   _____

5 Melany가 그녀의 사무실에 있다면, 그녀는 전화를 받을 것이다.

   _____

6 춥지 않다면, 우리는 바다에서 수영할 수 있다.

   _____

7 여분의 방이 하나 있다면, 너는 거기에서 머무를 수 있다.

   _____

8 그 티켓이 너무 비싸면, 나는 그 쇼에 갈 수 없다.

   _____

9 내가 Sarah의 생일 파티에 가지 않는다면, 그녀는 실망할 것이다. (unless)

   _____

10 네가 그 음식을 그 냉장고에 보관하지 않는다면, 그것은 상하게 될 것이다. (unless)

   _____

Unit 12 가정법 과거

 Writing에 필요한 문법

1. 가정법 과거의 형태

If+주어+동사의 과거형, 주어+조동사의 과거형+동사원형

2. 가정법 과거가 있는 문장 맛보기

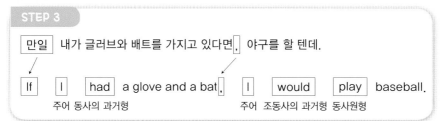

3. 가정법 과거의 쓰임

쓰임	예문	해석
현재 사실과 반대되는 상황을 가정	If I had **enough money**, I would buy **you a nice car.** If Paul didn't tell **a lie,** we would be **friends.** If she were(was) **a student,** she would study **hard.**	만일 –한다면, –할 텐데.

 참조

* If절에서 be동사의 과거는 1인칭과 3인칭에도 were를 사용하나, 일상회화에서는 was를 쓰기도 함.

If I were a doctor, I would take care of the sick people.

= If I was a doctor, I would take care of the sick people.

Writing에 필요한 문법 확인

A. 다음 중 알맞은 것을 고르시오.

1 If I (have / had) time, I could help you with your work.

2 If Serena liked to draw a picture, she (will / would) join our art club.

3 If I (were / be) you, I would throw him a surprise party.

4 If the bakery closed early, you (can't / couldn't) buy the bread.

5 If he (be / was) a pilot, he could travel to many different countries.

B. 주어진 단어를 이용하여 문장을 완성하시오.

1 If you _____ us, we would finish the project on time. (help)

2 If Jon _____ tired, he could give me a ride. (not, be)

3 If she was nice to me, I _____ her. (like)

4 If I were you, I _____ secrets to anyone. (not, tell)

5 If the shopping mall _____ near my house, I would buy you
   a dress. (be)

C. 가정법 과거 문장이 되도록 틀린 부분을 바르게 고치시오.

1 If my grandfather is still alive, I would visit him often.   _____

2 If David listened to your song, he will fall in love with you.   _____

3 If you don't drop the glass, it wouldn't break.   _____

4 If they weren't here, we can't move the heavy piano.   _____

5 If I am you, I would marry her.
   _____

English	Korean	English	Korean
autograph	n. 싸인	quickly	adv. 빨리
break one's leg	다리를 부러뜨리다	singer	n. 가수
careful	adj. 조심하는	soup	n. 수프
chocolate	n. 초콜릿	too	adv. 너무
dishwasher	n. 식기세척기	visit	v. 방문하다
healthy	adj. 건강한	wash dishes	설거지하다
plant	v. 심다	waste	v. 낭비하다

다음의 우리말 표현을 <u>가정법 과거시제</u>를 사용하여 영어로 쓰시오.

1 만일 내가 글러브와 배트를 가지고 있다면   if I had a glove and a bat

2 만일 나의 엄마가 지금 여기에 계시면   _____

3 만일 그 소년이 주의한다면   _____

4 만일 그가 집에 있다면   _____

5 만일 내가 식기세척기를 가지고 있다면   _____

6 만일 Kate가 그 가수를 만난다면   _____

7 만일 네가 너무 많은 초콜릿을 먹지 않는다면   _____

8 만일 내가 너라면   _____

9 만일 내가 많은 사과 나무들을 심는다면   _____

10 만일 네가 너의 일을 세 시까지 끝낸다면(by three)   _____

🐚 **다음의 우리말 표현을 영어로 쓰시오.**

1 나는   글러브와 배트를   가지고 있다.

   I   have   a glove and a bat.
   주어   동사   목적어

2 나의 엄마가   지금   여기에   계신다 .

   _____

3 그 소년은   주의한다 .

   _____

4 그는   집에   있다 .

   _____

5 나는   식기세척기를   가지고 있다 .

   _____

6 Kate는   그 가수를   만난다 .

   _____

7 너는   너무 많은 초콜릿을   먹지 않는다 .

   _____

8 나는   너이다 .

   _____

9 나는   많은 사과 나무들을   심는다 .

   _____

10 너는   세 시까지   너의 일을   끝낸다 .

   _____

🐚 **다음의 우리말 표현을 영어로 쓰시오.**

1 　나는　 야구를 　할 것이다.

　　↓　　　✕

　　I　 will play 　baseball.

　　주어　　동사　　　목적어

2 　그녀는　 나를 위해　 수프를　 만들 것이다 .

_____

3 　그는　 그의 다리를　 부러뜨리지 않을 것이다 .

_____

4 　나는　 그를　 방문할 것이다 .

_____

5 　나는　 설거지를　 빨리　 끝낼 수 있다 .

_____

6 　그녀는　 그의 싸인을　 받을 수 있다 .

_____

7 　너는　 건강해질 것이다 .

_____

8 　나는　 TV 보는데 (watching TV)　 시간을　 낭비하지 않을 것이다 .

_____

9 　나는　 더 많은 사과들을　 얻을 것이다 (get).

_____

10 　너는　 우리와 함께　 갈 수 있다 (come).

_____

🐚 **다음의 우리말 표현을 가정법 과거시제를 사용하여 영어로 쓰시오.**

1 만일 내가 글러브와 배트를 가지고 있다면, 야구를 할 텐데.

   If I had a glove and a bat, I would play baseball.

2 만일 나의 엄마가 지금 여기에 계시면, 나를 위해 수프를 만들어주실 텐데. (would)

   _____

3 만일 그 소년이 주의한다면, 그의 다리가 부러지지 않을 텐데. (would)

   _____

4 만일 그가 집에 있다면, 나는 그를 방문할 텐데. (would)

   _____

5 만일 내가 식기세척기를 가지고 있다면, 설거지를 빨리 끝낼 수 있을 텐데. (could)

   _____

6 만일 Kate가 그 가수를 만난다면, 그의 싸인을 받을 수 있을 텐데. (could)

   _____

7 만일 네가 너무 많은 초콜릿을 먹지 않는다면, 너는 건강할 텐데. (would)

   _____

8 만일 내가 너라면, 나는 TV 보는데 시간을 낭비하지 않을 텐데. (would)

   _____

9 만일 내가 많은 사과 나무들을 심는다면, 더 많은 사과들을 얻을 텐데. (would)

   _____

10 만일 네가 너의 일을 세 시까지 끝낸다면, 너는 우리와 함께 갈 수 있을 텐데. (could)

   _____

More Practice

A. 주어진 단어를 사용하여 문장을 완성하시오.

1 whose sons are teachers / next door to me / the woman / lives / .

_____

2 that / I borrowed / lost the book / from the library / I / .

_____

3 late / , / the bus / if / I will / take a taxi / arrives / .

_____

4 more workers / if / , / grew / would hire / my company / I / .

_____

B. 다음 문장을 영작하시오.

1 나는 그 서점에서 내가 원했던 책을 샀다. (buy, from the bookstore)

_____

2 노란 모자를 쓰고 있는 그 여자는 나의 수학 선생님이다. (wear a yellow hat)

_____

3 네가 일찍 오면, 너는 그 영화를 볼 수 있다. (can, watch the movie)

_____

4 내가 너라면, 나는 거기에 혼자 가지 않을 텐데. (would, go there alone)

_____

🐚 Sally가 지난 여름 휴가 때 찍은 사진을 친구들에게 보여주며 가족을 소개하고 있다. Sally가 휴가를 즐기던 중 작성한 글을 참고하여 문장을 완성하시오. (who, whose, whom, which, that이 모두 한 번씩 쓰여지도록 작성하시오.)

> I am at the beach with my family on summer vacation. We are having fun here. My puppy is happy, too. He is running on the beach all day. Dad is building a sandcastle. Mom is playing with my brother. They are playing with a ball. My brother can throw and catch a ball very well. I think that his arms are very strong.

Hello, my name is Sally. This is the picture <u>which I took</u> last summer vacation. Let's look at the picture. The man _____ is my dad. The woman _____ is my mom. The boy _____ is my brother. Can you find a puppy, too? Yes, the puppy _____ is my lovely pet.

Unit 1 사역동사

[Writing에 필요한 문법 확인]   p.7-8

A. 1 cut   2 stay up   3 make the bed
   4 fixed   5 jump

B. 1 to bark → bark   2 waited → wait
   3 to finish → finish   4 my → me
   5 steal → stolen

C. 1 let, lick   2 made, put
   3 had, cut   4 had, set the table
   5 let, talk loudly

[Warm Up : 표현 만들기]   p.8

2 They let their kids watch
3 The mom let her son play
4 Jenny has her car checked
5 Dad let me buy soccer shoes
6 Gina makes her students write
7 I made my kids eat
8 I had my students decorate
9 The airline let me switch
10 I had a company paint

[Step 1 : 문장 시작하기]   p.9

2 They let their kids watch TV.
3 The mom let her son play with their dog.
4 Jenny has her old car checked.
5 Dad let me buy brand-new soccer shoes.
6 Gina makes her students write a journal.
7 I made my kids eat vegetables.
8 I had my students decorate the classroom.
9 The airline let me switch my flight.
10 I had a company paint my house.

[Step 2 : 문장 완성하기]   p.10

2 They usually let their kids watch TV.
3 The mom let her son play with their cute dog.
4 Jenny always has her old car checked.
5 Dad let me buy brand-new soccer shoes for

the practice .
6 Gina makes her students write a journal every day .
7 I made my kids eat all the vegetables.
8 I had my students decorate the classroom with colored paper .
9 The airline let me switch my flight without a penalty .
10 I had a company paint my new house.

[Step 3 : 문장 꾸미기]   p.11

2 They usually let their kids watch TV after finishing their homework .
3 The mom let her son play with their cute dog in the backyard .
4 Jenny always has her old car checked regularly .
5 Dad let me buy brand-new soccer shoes for the practice yesterday .
6 Gina makes her students write a journal every day during vacation .
7 I made my kids eat all the vegetables on the plate .
8 I had my students decorate the classroom with colored paper for Halloween .
9 Fortunately , the airline let me switch my flight without a penalty .
10 I had a company paint my new house in Seattle .

Unit 2 동명사 1 (주어)

[Writing에 필요한 문법 확인]   p.13

A. 1 Listening to music
   2 Eating delicious food
   3 Drawing pictures
   4 Exercising
   5 Buying the house

B. 1 is   2 keeps   3 is   4 makes   5 is

C. 1 Singing   2 doesn't burn   3 is

4 Shopping   5 takes

[Warm Up : 표현 만들기]   p.14

2 gardening

3 speaking English

4 studying abroad

5 listening to music

6 walking up the stairs in the building

7 storing vegetables

8 watching this movie

9 taking an airplane

10 learning a new language

[Step 1 : 문장 시작하기]   p.15

2 Gardening became my hobby.

3 Speaking English can be challenging.

4 Studying abroad was the best experience.

5 Listening to classical music helps me.

6 Walking up the stairs in the building keeps you healthy.

7 Storing vegetables keeps them fresh.

8 Watching this movie reminds me of my childhood.

9 Taking an airplane makes me sick.

10 Learning a new language is useful.

[Step 2 : 문장 완성하기]   p.16

2 Gardening became my favorite hobby.

3 Speaking English can be very challenging.

4 Studying abroad was one of the best experiences.

5 Listening to classical music helps me to stay relaxed .

6 Walking up the stairs in the tall building keeps you healthy.

7 Storing vegetables in the fridge keeps them fresh.

8 Watching this movie reminds me of my childhood in the village .

9 Taking an airplane makes me sick because of the low pressure .

10 Learning a new language is useful for traveling abroad .

[Step 3 : 문장 꾸미기]   p.17

2 Gardening became my favorite hobby after we moved into the new house .

3 Speaking English can be very challenging in some situations .

4 Studying abroad was one of the best experiences of my life .

5 Listening to classical music helps me to stay very relaxed.

6 Walking up the stairs instead of riding the elevator in the tall building keeps you healthy.

7 Storing vegetables in the fridge keeps them fresh for quite some time .

8 Watching this movie reminds me of my childhood in the mountain village.

9 Taking an airplane makes me sick because of the low pressure on the plane .

10 Learning a new language is quite useful for traveling abroad.

🌸3 동명사 2 (목적어)

[Writing에 필요한 문법 확인]   p.19-20

A. 1 to do   2 jogging   3 ignoring
    4 talking   5 making

B. 1 swimming   2 to see   3 closing   4 using
    5 reading

C. 1 reading   2 to visit   3 to join
    4 to bring   5 calling

[Warm Up : 표현 만들기]   p.20

2 finished grooming her fur

3 enjoy going for relaxing walks

4 suggest studying

5 mind closing the big window

6 gave up waiting for her

7 stopped barking at the door

8 postponed throwing a party

9 enjoy eating vegetables

10 avoided talking with me

[Step 1 : 문장 시작하기]   p.21

2 My cat finished grooming her fur.

3 My family enjoys going for relaxing walks.

4 I suggest studying English.

5 Do you mind closing the big window?

6 He gave up waiting for her.

7 My dog stopped barking at the door.

8 We postponed throwing a party for Gina.

9 I enjoy eating vegetables.

10 My friend Jenny avoided talking with me.

[Step 2 : 문장 완성하기]   p.22

2 My cat finished grooming her soft fur.

3 My family enjoys going for relaxing walks in the afternoon .

4 I suggest studying English every day .

5 Do you mind closing the big window next to the vase ?

6 He gave up waiting for her after many hours .

7 My dog stopped barking at the front door.

8 We postponed throwing a birthday party for Gina.

9 I enjoy eating fresh vegetables.

10 My friend Jenny avoided talking with me after the fight .

[Step 3 : 문장 꾸미기]   p.23

2 My cat finished grooming her soft fur before going to bed .

3 My family enjoys going for relaxing walks in the afternoon on sunny days .

4 I suggest studying English every day before the test .

5 Do you mind closing the big window next to the white vase?

6 He gave up waiting for her after many hours at the mall .

7 My dog finally stopped barking at the front door.

8 We postponed throwing a birthday party for Gina yesterday .

9 I enjoy eating fresh vegetables with pizza .

10 My friend Jenny avoided talking with me after the big fight .

Check Up 1. Unit 1-3

[More Practice]   p.24

A. 1 I had my son wash the dishes after breakfast.

2 Watching action movies helps me to release stress.

3 My parents enjoy climbing a rocky mountain on weekdays.

4 I usually let my kittens play on the bed.

B. 1 I like reading books on various subjects in my free time.

2 Taking photos of dogs is my hobby.

3 We made Dad mop the floor and clean the bathroom.

4 They didn't let their kids play in the rain.

[Creative Thinking Activity]   p.25

1 riding a bicycle

2 watching TV (to watch TV) / reading books (to read books)

3 cleaning his room (to clean his room)

4 to be a scientist

4 동명사 3 (보어, 전치사의 목적어)

[Writing에 필요한 문법 확인]   p.27-28

A. 1 teaching   2 Reading   3 waiting
   4 leaving   5 buying

B. 1 fixing   2 cleaning   3 getting up
   4 becoming   5 receiving

C. 1 making   2 playing   3 going
   4 traveling   5 helping

[Warm Up : 표현 만들기]   p.28

2 fixing cars   3 playing games
4 reading books   5 after getting up
6 before leaving   7 without finishing
8 hearing from you   9 making breakfast
10 helping the poor

[Step 1 : 문장 시작하기]   p.29

2 My job is fixing cars.
3 The boy's hobby is playing games.
4 My favorite thing to do is reading books.
5 She drinks water after getting up.
6 Make sure to lock the door before leaving.
7 The kids cannot go on a picnic without
   finishing.
8 We look forward to hearing from you.
9 Dad is used to making breakfast.
10 The nurse was committed to helping the
   poor.

[Step 2 : 문장 완성하기]   p.30

2 My job is fixing cars and motorcycles.
3 The boy's hobby is playing computer games.
4 My favorite thing to do in the afternoon is
   reading books.
5 She always drinks water after getting up.
6 Make sure to lock the front door before
   leaving.
7 The kids cannot go on a picnic without
   finishing homework.
8 We very much look forward to hearing from
   you.
9 Dad is used to making breakfast and
   cleaning the house.
10 The nurse was committed to helping the
   poor and the sick.

[Step 3 : 문장 꾸미기]   p.31

2 My main job is fixing cars and motorcycles.
3 The boy's favorite hobby is playing
   computer games.
4 My favorite thing to do in the afternoon is
   reading books in the sun.
5 She always drinks cold water after getting
   up.
6 Make sure to lock the front door before
   leaving the house.
7 The kids cannot go on a picnic at the park
   without finishing homework.
8 We very much look forward to hearing from
   you soon.
9 Dad is used to making breakfast and cleaning
   the house during his summer vacation.
10 The nurse was committed to helping the
   poor and the sick in Africa.

Unit 5 현재분사

[Writing에 필요한 문법 확인]   p.33

A. 1 Did you see the man (cleaning) the windows
     of the tall building?
   2 The boy (swimming) in the pool is my son.
   3 I like to visit a museum (showing) Korean
     history.
   4 (Melting) snow will make the road dirty.
   5 The man (relaxing) on the couch is my
     husband.
B. 1 The v water in the kettle is making sound.
   2 The kitten is v on the couch.
   3 Look at the beautiful rainbow v up in the
     sky.
   4 The man v on stage is my brother.
   5 They like to watch their dogs v in the
     backyard.
C. 1 The woman washing the dishes in the
     kitchen is my wife.
   2 Those flowers floating on water over
     there are lilies.

3 That puppy playing with the ball is only five months old.

4 The man cleaning the bathroom floor is my father.

5 The cat making a loud sound is scared.

[Warm Up : 표현 만들기]   p.34

2 the stars shining in the sky

3 the sleeping puppy

4 the ducks floating on the pond

5 the boiling water

6 the soup cooking in the kitchen

7 the man walking toward me

8 art galleries showing paintings of animals

9 their kids playing in the park

10 the swing hanging from the tree

[Step 1 : 문장 시작하기]   p.35

2 Look at the beautiful stars!

3 The sleeping puppy is cute.

4 The ducks floating on the pond are friends.

5 The boiling water can make the house warm.

6 The soup cooking in the kitchen smells delicious.

7 The man walking toward me is my younger brother.

8 I like to visit art galleries.

9 They love to watch their kids playing.

10 It looks dangerous to play on the swing.

[Step 2 : 문장 완성하기]   p.36

2 Look at the beautiful stars shining in the sky !

3 The sleeping puppy is very cute.

4 The white ducks floating on the pond are friends.

5 The boiling water on the stove can make the house warm.

6 The mushroom soup cooking in the kitchen smells delicious.

7 The man walking toward me on the street is

my younger brother.

8 I like to visit art galleries showing paintings of animals .

9 They love to watch their kids playing in the park .

10 It looks dangerous to play on the old swing.

[Step 3 : 문장 꾸미기]   p.37

2 Look at the beautiful stars shining in the night sky!

3 The sleeping puppy on the couch is very cute.

4 The white ducks floating on the pond are the swan's friends.

5 The boiling water on the stove can make the house warm in the winter .

6 The mushroom soup cooking in the kitchen smells very (so) delicious.

7 The man walking toward me on the busy street is my younger brother.

8 I like to visit art galleries showing paintings of animals in Africa .

9 They love to watch their kids playing in the park near their house .

10 It looks dangerous to play on the old swing hanging from the tree .

6 과거분사

[Writing에 필요한 문법 확인]   p.39-40

A. 1 spoken   2 hidden   3 waiting   4 sent

5 painting

B. 1 confused → confusing

2 interested → interesting

3 exciting → excited

4 surprising → surprised

5 disappointed → disappointing

C. 2 locked door   3 endangered animals

4 singing girls   5 lost wallet

2 an abandoned dog　　3 embarrassed

4 the shattered glass　　5 excited

6 disappointed　　　　　7 the parked van

8 confused　　　　　　　9 fallen leaves

10 the broken door

[Step 1 : 문장 시작하기]　　　　p.41

2 I found a dog.

3 Tina was embarrassed.

4 The glass is dangerous.

5 I am excited.

6 They were disappointed.

7 The van is my uncle's.

8 The students are confused.

9 My hobby is collecting leaves.

10 He fixed the door.

[Step 2 : 문장 완성하기]　　　　p.42

2 I found an abandoned dog.

3 Tina was embarrassed by the questions.

4 The shattered glass is dangerous.

5 I am excited about meeting new people.

6 They were disappointed by the election result.

7 The parked van is my uncle's.

8 The students are confused by the theory.

9 My hobby is collecting fallen leaves.

10 He fixed the broken door.

[Step 3 : 문장 꾸미기]　　　　p.43

2 I found an abandoned dog in the park.

3 Tina was really embarrassed by the questions.

4 The shattered glass is dangerous to children.

5 I am always excited about meeting new people.

6 To be honest, they were disappointed by the election result.

7 The parked van in the parking lot is my uncle's.

8 The students are confused by the complex theory.

9 My hobby is collecting fallen leaves in autumn.

10 He fixed the broken door made of steel.

Check Up 2. Unit 4-6

[More Practice]　　　　p.44

A. 1 Mom is used to solving difficult math questions.

　2 Their dream is to live in a beautiful town by the beach.

　3 The girl eating chocolate ice cream is my sister.

　4 I cannot exchange the tickets purchased on the Internet.

B. 1 Please make sure to close the windows before leaving.

　2 There is a book written by a famous writer on the desk.

　3 The swans floating on the water are very beautiful.

　4 My job is taking care of animals at the park.

[Creative Thinking Activity]　　　　p.45

1 washing(doing) the dishes

2 wearing a hat

3 swimming at the beach

4 riding a motorcycle

5 wearing glasses

⑦ 명사절

[Writing에 필요한 문법 확인]　　　　p.47

A. 1 Do you know ∨ some large frogs even eat small snakes?

　2 It's true ∨ there are many tall buildings in

our city.

3 I think v Cindy is the most famous actress in my country.

4 It is a fact v the Earth is getting warmer.

5 It is true v the novel was written by a young boy.

B. 1 if   2 Whether   3 that   4 It
5 whether

C. 1 It is very surprising that Jon wants to be a pilot.

2 I asked Mr. Kim if he booked a ticket for Seattle.

3 I am not sure whether Dad will come home late tonight.

[Warm Up : 표현 만들기]　　　　　　p.48

2 that Anna and John will get married

3 whether(if) he needs our help

4 whether(if) this bus goes to downtown

5 that Mr. Kim can't speak Japanese

6 that Tyler plans to buy a new car

7 whether(if) the woman is over 40 years old

8 that he got a driver's license

9 that we did our best

10 whether(if) Tom will take her to the airport

[Step 1 : 문장 시작하기]　　　　　　p.49

2 I heard.　　　　　3 We don't know.

4 Tell me.　　　　　5 It's true.

6 Is it a fact?　　　　7 Do you know?

8 It's not surprising.　9 It's important.

10 Kelly wonders.

[Step 2 : 문장 완성하기]　　　　　　p.50

2 Anna and John will get married.

3 He needs our help.

4 This bus goes to downtown.

5 Mr. Kim can't speak Japanese.

6 Tyler plans to buy a new car.

7 The woman is over 40 years old.

8 He got a driver's license.

9 We did our best.

10 Tom will take her to the airport.

[Step 3 : 문장 꾸미기]　　　　　　p.51

2 I heard (that) Anna and John will get married.

3 We don't know whether(if) he needs our help.

4 Tell me whether(if) this bus goes to downtown.

5 It's true that Mr. Kim can't speak Japanese.

6 Is it a fact that Tyler plans to buy a new car?

7 Do you know whether(if) the woman is over 40 years old?

8 It's not surprising that he got a driver's license.

9 It's important that we did our best.

10 Kelly wonders whether(if) Tom will take her to the airport.

🌩 8 부사절

[Writing에 필요한 문법 확인]　　　　p.53-54

A. 1 When fall comes, leaves begin to change color.

2 x

3 Even though it rained heavily, the girl didn't wear her rain boots.

4 Because I didn't sleep well last night, I'm very tired.

5 x

B. 1 before   2 Because   3 even though
4 When   5 while

C. 1 even though   2 Because   3 Even though
4 because   5 even though

[Warm Up : 표현 만들기]　　　　　　p.54

2 when you called me last night

3 while you are cleaning the house

4 before you go to bed

5 because he studied hard

6 because it's very cold

7 while I was reading a book

8 even though the weather was not good

9 even though my grandmother is 70 years old

10 after you do your homework

[Step 1 : 문장 시작하기] p.55

2 You called me last night.

3 You are cleaning the house.

4 You should brush your teeth.

5 He got a good grade on the exam.

6 She wears a coat.

7 Mom made dinner.

8 The weather was not good.

9 My grandmother is 70 years old.

10 You can play outside.

[Step 2 : 문장 완성하기] p.56

2 I was listening to music.

3 I will wash the dishes.

4 You go to bed.

5 He studied hard.

6 It's very cold.

7 I was reading a book.

8 We went on a picnic.

9 She looks very young.

10 You do your homework.

[Step 3 : 문장 꾸미기] p.57

2 When you called me last night, I was listening to music.

3 While you are cleaning the house, I will wash the dishes.

4 You should brush your teeth before you go to bed.

5 He got a good grade on the exam because he studied hard.

6 She wears a coat because it's very cold.

7 Mom made dinner while I was reading a book.

8 Even though the weather was not good, we went on a picnic.

9 Even though my grandmother is 70 years old, she looks very young.

10 You can play outside after you do your homework.

🟦 Unit 9 과거완료

[Writing에 필요한 문법 확인] p.59-60

A. 1 had brushed   2 had left   3 had studied
   4 had taught   5 had visited

B. 1 had, left   2 had lived   3 had sent
   4 had been   5 had read

C. 1 After Sarah had stopped drinking coffee, she could sleep well.

   2 When I arrived in the classroom, the lecture had started.

   3 Jason had read the book when his mom called him.

[Warm Up : 표현 만들기] p.60

2 I had studied

3 Jack had been a baseball player

4 They had not believed

5 Sarah had bought

6 David had learned

7 Mike had lived

8 My dog had broken

9 Jason had spent

10 Jay had studied

[Step 1 : 문장 시작하기] p.61

2 I took the math test.

3 Jack became a businessman.

4 They observed it.

5 I arrived at the theater.

6 David learned Korean.

7 He earned a lot of money.

8 I woke up.

9 His mom called him.

10 Jay studied physics.

[Step 2 : 문장 완성하기]   p.62

2 I studied math very hard.

3 Jack was a famous baseball player.

4 They didn't believe the surprising truth.

5 Sarah bought tickets at the box office.

6 He began to understand Korean culture.

7 Mike lived in a small house.

8 My dog broke the expensive vase.

9 Jason already spent all his money.

10 Jay studied biology for years.

[Step 3 : 문장 꾸미기]   p.63

2 Before I took the math test, I had studied math very hard.

3 Before Jack bacame a businessman, he had been a famous baseball player.

4 Before they observed it, they had not believed the surprising truth.

5 When I arrived at the theater, Sarah had bought tickets at the box office.

6 After David had learned Korean, he began to understand Korean culture.

7 Before Mike earned a lot of money, he had lived in a small house.

8 Before I woke up, my dog had broken the expensive vase.

9 When Jason's mom called Jason, he had already spent all his money.

10 Before Jay studied physics, he had studied biology for years.

Check Up 3. Unit 7-9

[More Practice]   p.64

A. 1 It's not obvious whether we will have a White Christmas this year.

2 Is it a fact that James had a car accident last night?

3 Even though the weather is not good, I will enjoy swimming.

4 When we got home, they had already eaten dinner.

B. 1 I wonder whether Jon loves Julie.

2 Tom heard (that) she will leave for England.

3 Mr. Homer ran a famous restaurant when he lived in Italy.

4 Sharon found that she had left her bag at the restaurant.

[Creative Thinking Activity]   p.65

② After I washed my hands, I ate dinner with my family.

③ I was doing my homework while my mom was washing the dishes.

④ I had to do my homework again because he messed up my homework.

⑤ Even though I was angry with him, I still love my little brother.

Unit 10 관계대명사

[Writing에 필요한 문법 확인]   p.67-68

A. 1 whose   2 who   3 that   4 that
5 whom

B. 1 I like the woman who teaches me science at school.

2 Can you tell me about your new computer which you bought yesterday?

3 The movie that I saw last week was fun and touching.

4 The bus driver who took us to school is very kind.

5 The people whom I met at the mall were friendly.

[Warm Up : 표현 만들기]

2 (which/that) Tom recommended to me

3 who is wearing glasses

4 (whom/that) I like

5 (which/that) we discussed

6 whose food is delicious

7 whose sister is a famous singer

8 (which/that) my father grew

9 who enjoys reading

10 whose name is Happy

[Step 1 : 문장 시작하기] p.69

2 I will go to the beach.

3 The boy is my brother.

4 The swimmer won a gold medal.

5 The topic was interesting.

6 Do you know any restaurant?

7 I ran into an old friend.

8 The apples were perfectly ripe.

9 The man is a vegetarian.

10 Jane has a puppy.

[Step 2 : 문장 완성하기] p.70

2 Tom recommended it to me.

3 He is wearing glasses.

4 I like him.

5 We discussed it yesterday.

6 Its food is delicious.

7 His sister is a famous singer.

8 My father grew them.

9 He enjoys reading.

10 Her name is Happy.

[Step 3 : 문장 꾸미기] p.71

2 I will go to the beach (which/that) Tom recommended to me.

3 The boy who is wearing glasses is my brother.

4 The swimmer (whom/that) I like won a gold medal.

5 The topic (which/that) we discussed

yesterday was interesting.

6 Do you know any restaurant whose food is delicious?

7 I ran into an old friend whose sister is a famous singer.

8 The apples (which/that) my father grew were perfectly ripe.

9 The man who enjoys reading is a vegetarian.

10 Jane has a puppy whose name is Happy.

Unit 11 가정법 현재

[Writing에 필요한 문법 확인] p.73

A. 1 hurries　　2 take　3 doesn't drive

　　4 don't submit　　5 is

B. 1 doesn't rain → rains / Unless → If

　　2 hear → hears　　3 didn't → don't

　　4 don't follow → follow / Unless → If

　　5 didn't → won't

C. 1 miss　　2 practices　　3 stand　　4 goes

　　5 come

[Warm Up : 표현 만들기] p.74

2 if the weather is good

3 if Mrs. Kim has enough apples

4 if I have some tools

5 if Melany is in her office

6 if it is not cold

7 if there is an extra room

8 if the ticket is too expensive

9 unless I go to Sarah's birthday party

10 unless you keep the food in the refrigerator

[Step 1 : 문장 시작하기] p.75

2 The weather is good.

3 Mrs. Kim has enough apples.

4 I have some tools.

5 Melany is in her office.

6 It is not cold.

7 There is an extra room.

8 The ticket is too expensive.

9 I go to Sarah's birthday party.

10 You keep the food in the refrigerator.

[Step 2 : 문장 완성하기]   p.76

2 We won't cancel the trip.

3 She will make apple jam.

4 I can fix your bicycle.

5 She will answer the phone.

6 We can swim in the sea.

7 You can stay there.

8 I can't go to the show.

9 She will be disappointed.

10 It will be spoiled.

[Step 3 : 문장 꾸미기]   p.77

2 If the weather is good, we won't cancel the trip.

3 If Mrs. Kim has enough apples, she will make apple jam.

4 If I have some tools, I can fix your bicycle.

5 If Melany is in her office, she will answer the phone.

6 If it is not cold, we can swim in the sea.

7 If there is an extra room, you can stay there.

8 If the ticket is too expensive, I can't go to the show.

9 Unless I go to Sarah's birthday party, she will be disappointed.

10 Unless you keep the food in the refrigerator, it will be spoiled.

Unit 12 가정법 과거

[Writing에 필요한 문법 확인]   p.79

A. 1 had   2 would   3 were   4 couldn't

5 was

B. 1 helped   2 weren't(wasn't)

3 would like   4 wouldn't tell

5 were(was)

C. 1 is → were(was)   2 will → would

3 don't → didn't   4 can't → couldn't

5 am → were(was)

[Warm Up : 표현 만들기]   p.80

2 if my mom were(was) here now

3 if the boy were(was) careful

4 if he were(was) at home

5 if I had a dishwasher

6 if Kate met the singer

7 if you didn't eat too much chocolate

8 if I were(was) you

9 if I planted many apple trees

10 if you finished your work by three

[Step 1 : 문장 시작하기]   p.81

2 My mom is here now.

3 The boy is careful.

4 He is at home.

5 I have a dishwasher.

6 Kate meets the singer.

7 You don't eat too much chocolate.

8 I am you.

9 I plant many apple trees.

10 You finish your work by three.

[Step 2 : 문장 완성하기]   p.82

2 She will make soup for me.

3 He won't break his leg.

4 I will visit him.

5 I can finish washing dishes quickly.

6 She can get his autograph.

7 You will be healthy.

8 I won't waste time watching TV.

9 I will get more apples.

10 You can come with us.

[Step 3 : 문장 꾸미기]   p.83

2 If my mom were(was) here now, she would make soup for me.

3 If the boy were(was) careful, he wouldn't break his leg.

4 If he were(was) at home, I would visit him.

5 If I had a dishwasher, I could finish washing dishes quickly.

6 If Kate met the singer, she could get his autograph.

7 If you didn't eat too much chocolate, you would be healthy.

8 If I were(was) you, I wouldn't waste time watching TV.

9 If I planted many apple trees, I would get more apples.

10 If you finished your work by three, you could come with us.

Check Up 4. Unit 10-12

[More Practice]   p.84

A. 1 The woman whose sons are teachers lives next door to me.

 2 I lost the book that I borrowed from the library.

 3 If the bus arrives late, I will take a taxi.

 4 If my company grew, I would hire more workers.

B. 1 I bought the book (which/that) I wanted from the bookstore.

 2 The woman who is wearing a yellow hat is my math teacher.

 3 If you come early, you can watch the movie.

 4 If I were(was) you, I would not go there alone.

[Creative Thinking Activity]   p.85

   Hello, my name is Sally. This is the picture which I took last summer vacation. Let's look at the picture. The man who is building a sandcastle is my dad. The woman who(m) my brother is playing with is my mom. The boy whose arms are very strong is my brother. Can you find a puppy, too? Yes, the puppy that is running on the beach is my lovely pet.